RUBY'S
LOW-FAT
SOUL FOOD
COOKBOOK

RUBY'S LOW-FAT SOUL FOOD COOKBOOK

Ruby Banks-Payne

CONTEMPORARY BOOKS

A TRIBUNE COMPANY

Library of Congress Cataloging-in-Publication Data

Banks-Payne, Ruby.
    Ruby's low-fat soul food cookbook / Ruby Banks-Payne.
        p.   cm.
    Includes index.
    ISBN 0-8092-3153-0
    1. Afro-American cookery.   2. Cookery, Cajun.   3. Cookery, Creole.
    4. Low-fat diet—Recipes.   I. Title.
    TX715.B22   1996
    641.59'296073—dc20   96-15855
                                                    CIP

Cover design by Monica Baziuk
Author photo by Curtis Johnson/Arndt Photography Inc.
Interior design by Mary Lockwood

Published by Contemporary Books
An imprint of NTC/Contemporary Publishing Company
Two Prudential Plaza, Chicago, Illinois 60601-6790
Manufactured in the United States of America
International Standard Book Number: 0-8092-3153-0

10   9   8   7   6   5   4   3   2   1

With all my heart and soul I dedicate this to my children—Darren, Leslie, and Chad. I hope that through healthy eating habits that include traditional "soul foods" their heritage will not be forgotten.

I am indebted to the generations of great cooks who came before me. Through this book my hopes are for a healthier generation that can appreciate low-fat soul food and integrate it into everyday living.

Let the recipes that follow carry forth our traditions in new and healthier dishes *rediscovered*.

Contents

Acknowledgments IX

Introduction: Our Food History XI

1. Soups, Stews, and Gumbos 1

2. Salads 25

3. Beans, Beans, and More Beans 33

4. Main Courses 45

5. Vegetables 77

6. Biscuits and Breads 101

7. Desserts 123

8. Seasoning Blends, Dressings, Sauces,

    and Toppings 147

9. Beverages 163

Index 171

Acknowledgments

T hanks to my supportive friends Nancy Walters, Nancy Schiller, Gwen Trinity, and Maria Huerta–Lopez, without whose continuing support this book would not exist.

Thanks also to my extended family, with love.

INTRODUCTION: OUR FOOD HISTORY

WHAT IS SOUL FOOD?

African Americans refer to soul food as "food that sticks to your ribs," food that makes you pull back from the dinner table completely satisfied. Soul food includes the traditional dishes that native Africans brought to the New World. Soul food is part of our heritage, a mainstay in our rich culture to this day.

In 1619, the first Africans landed in America at Jamestown, Virginia. These slaves cooked a variety of meals, usually consisting of cabbage, corn, ashcakes, sweet potatoes, yams, and hominy. Later, additional foods such as crab cakes, succotash, pones, greens, and spoonbread were added to their repertoire. For the most part, cooking was done over an open fireplace.

In the 1860s, during the Civil War, Creole and Cajun cooking were developed. New dishes–gumbo, red beans and rice, dirty rice, bread pudding, and jambalaya—also became mainstays of soul food cuisine. Throughout the 1860s and 1870s, a number of other foods were introduced to our culture as soul food, and these dishes are what comes to mind for many people when "soul food" is mentioned: candied yams, black-eyed peas, pig's feet, okra, fried chicken, and chitlins. All of these have been enjoyed in African American homes for generations. In recent years, however, an increased awareness of the role these high-fat, high-calorie, cholesterol-laden foods play in diseases such as diabetes, high blood pressure, and heart disease has led to the development of new cooking techniques for these much-loved traditional foods.

The goal of this book is to allow each of us to maintain good health while exploring our food heritage. Traditional soul food recipes use far too much fat, sugar, and sodium for good health. By reducing fat, sugar, and sodium (traditional, but unnecessary, components in these dishes), we can truly nourish our souls with a rich culinary history while also nourishing our bodies with healthful and delicious foods.

Although this book was developed to keep the tradition of African American cookery alive, there remain certain foods that are simply not nutritional. These foods are:

• chitlins
• ham hocks
• neckbones
• pig's feet

These foods have been eliminated from this book. To share traditional foods that are high in fat with our children's children is OK. A single celebratory meal yearly (preferably during Kwanzaa) is enough to let them know what and how earlier generations cooked.

A healthy diet reduces our chances of developing high blood pressure, heart disease, stroke, certain cancers, and many common types of diabetes that plague African Americans. A diet low in fat not only helps reduce the risk of developing these diseases, but also helps us maintain a healthy body weight.

This cookbook contains more than 140 recipes for delicious, healthful versions of traditional soul food dishes. Many are updated versions of old family recipes passed down from generation to generation. The main meals re-created here are based on Cajun and Creole cooking. Cajun and Creole foods are French in origin, but they are often seasoned with Indian herbs and Spanish spices. Most Cajun recipes are prepared using a one-pot, slow-cooking technique that is a hallmark of African American cuisine.

A Few Simple Dietary Guidelines

- Eat a variety of foods to get the energy, protein, minerals, vitamins, and fiber your body needs on a daily basis to maintain good health.
- Maintain a healthy weight.
- Choose foods that are low in fat, cholesterol, sodium, and sugar.
- Eat plenty of vegetables, fruits, and grains.
- Choose low-fat dairy products.
- Select lean meats and skinless poultry.
- Enjoy fish as an entree several times a week.
- Eat in moderation.
- Develop and use low-fat cooking techniques.
- Choose broiled or roasted entrees when dining out.
- Do not add additional fats (such as butter) to cooked food.
- Limit your alcohol consumption. Nutritionally speaking, alcohol is nothing but empty calories.

Fats

The average American eats a diet in which more than 30 percent of the calories consumed come from fat. Current dietary guidelines recommend a goal of 25 percent. Saturated fat should be limited to less than 10 percent of total daily calories.

The following are particularly high in saturated fatty acids and should be avoided:

- beef fat
- butter
- cocoa butter
- coconut oil

- cream
- lard
- other meats high in fats
- palm kernel oil
- palm oil

The following oils are lower in saturated fatty acids and may be used *sparingly*:

- canola oil
- corn oil
- cottonseed oil
- olive oil
- peanut oil
- safflower oil
- sesame oil
- soybean oil
- sunflower oil

Reduce the Fat in Your Meals

Here are some commonly used ingredients and tasty, nutritious, low-fat substitutes for them:

HIGH-FAT FOOD	LOW-FAT SUBSTITUTE
whole milk (1 cup)	1 cup skim or low-fat milk plus 1 tablespoon unsaturated oil
heavy cream (1 cup)	1 cup evaporated skim milk
	or
	½ cup low-fat yogurt and ½ cup low-fat cottage cheese
sour cream	low-fat cottage cheese plus low-fat yogurt
	or

HIGH-FAT FOOD	LOW-FAT SUBSTITUTE
	chilled evaporated skim milk whipped with 1 teaspoon lemon juice
	or
	low-fat buttermilk
	or
	fat-free sour cream
cream cheese	fat-free cream cheese
egg (1)	2 egg whites

A Word About Sugar

Sugar goes by a variety of names. Corn sweetener, dextrose, fructose, honey, lactose, maltose, mannitol, molasses, sorbitol, sucrose, and syrup—these are some of the common terms for sugar in packaged foods. Sugar has very limited nutritional value and should be eaten in moderation to help prevent various afflictions such as obesity, diabetes mellitus, heart disease, and hyperactive behavior in young children. Cutting back on sugar is a good way to reduce the calories in your diet without reducing nutrients.

A Pinch of Salt

High blood pressure is related to diets that include high levels of sodium. Reducing the intake of salt and sodium will help individuals with high blood pressure live a longer life.

Many health experts recommend limiting sodium to 2,400 to 3,000 milligrams a day. Most Americans, however, consume 4,000—6,000 milligrams of sodium each day.

1 teaspoon salt = 2,325 milligrams sodium

½ teaspoon salt = 1,160 milligrams sodium

¼ teaspoon salt = 580 milligrams sodium

Almost anyone can benefit from decreasing salt intake. Start by not adding salt to foods at the table. You can also easily decrease the amount of salt called for in a recipe by substituting flavorful herbs and spices such as garlic or lemon pepper.

Some Benefits from These Recipes

Despite some of the health issues related to soul food's traditionally high fat and sugar content, many of these recipes contain ingredients that are currently highly recommended as being part of a healthful diet. For example, collard greens are an excellent source of vitamins A and C as well as calcium and iron. Mustard greens are also good sources of vitamins A and C, and thiamin and riboflavin. Greens such as these are also claimed to have cancer–fighting properties, acting to inhibit the spread of free radicals in the body. Rice and beans, which are commonly used together, provide a complete source of protein.

1
SOUPS, STEWS, AND GUMBOS

Court Bouillon

Fish Stock

Chicken Broth

Beef Stock

Black-Eyed Pea Soup

Crab Soup

Shrimp Soup

Bouillabaisse

Chicken Vegetable Soup

Corn Chowder

Country Chicken Chowder

Cajun Catfish Stew

Catfish Stew

Chicken Curry Stew

Catfish Gumbo

Codfish Gumbo

Seafood Gumbo

Quick Gumbo

Southern Okra and Crab Gumbo

Bonnie's Southern Chili

1

SOUPS

A soup's base may be anything from a thick broth to plain water. Soups can contain any combination of meat, poultry, fish, and vegetables. Making soup provides a good opportunity to clean out the refrigerator. Soups can be either the main course of a light meal or the first course of a larger meal, and are satisfying without being too filling. This quality makes soups particularly appropriate for warm-weather meals.

STEWS

Stews are often thought of as thickened soups. Their heartier character makes them ideal for one-course meals, particularly in cold-weather months. Stews are thickened either by reducing the broth that results from cooking or by adding flour. A perfect accompaniment to stew is a hearty, crusty bread.

STOCK

When preparing stock, always use the freshest ingredients possible. If you start with mediocre ingredients, you'll end up with mediocre stock. Making stock is a time-consuming task, but it's worth every minute. As a weekend project, you can make several different types of stock and freeze them for future use. The following tips should lead to successful stock-making.

- Always start with cold water. Hot tap water may contain minerals that could affect the flavor or your stock.
- Never add salt to stock until you use it. The recipe to which you add the stock may already include salt (in canned tomatoes, for example).
- If your stock seems too weak, boil it down to make it more concentrated.
- To avoid spoilage, proper cooling is very important. Strain hot stock into small containers, and place the containers in a sink of cold

water. Change the water as it becomes warm. Never put hot stock directly in the refrigerator.

• Before adding herbs to stock, refrigerate the stock to solidify the fat that rises to the surface. Then skim the surface to remove all of the visible fat.

• Use refrigerated stock within two days, or freeze it for up to six months.

GUMBO

There are many different types of gumbo, but the cooking techniques involved are usually the same. Traditional gumbos begin with a roux base most often made with butter. In the low-fat gumbo recipes included here, the roux is made with a reduced amount of fat or with stock. Either method will produce the desired thickness without undesired fat. Some gumbos are thickened with okra or filé, a powder made from dried sassafras leaves and originally discovered by the Choctaw Indians.

The most common gumbo ingredients are crab, chicken, shrimp, and sausage, although there are no real rules about what goes into gumbo. A good roux, some okra or filé powder, lots of chopped seasoning (usually onions, celery, peppers, and parsley), plus a little imagination will create an African American treat tantalizing enough to please any soul food lover.

COURT BOUILLON

1½ quarts cold water
2 cups dry white wine
1 lemon, sliced thin
1 medium carrot, sliced thick
1 medium onion, sliced thick

2 cloves garlic, chopped coarse
2 bay leaves
½ teaspoon celery seed
½ teaspoon whole peppercorns
2 tablespoons fresh lemon juice

Combine all ingredients in a large stockpot and bring to a boil. Reduce heat and simmer, uncovered, for 50 minutes. Strain into clean containers and refrigerate or freeze.

Use court bouillon for cooking seafood such as shrimp, crab, lobster, and crawfish, or for poaching fish.

Makes about 6 cups bouillon

Nutritional Information per Serving (based on 6 servings)

Calories • 56	Calories from Fat • 0	Percent of Calories from Fat • 0%	Fat • 0g
Protein • 1g	Carbohydrate • 1.3g	Cholesterol • 0mg	Sodium • 11mg

Fish Stock

2 pounds fish heads, bones, and trimmings

2½ quarts cold water

3 medium onions, chopped coarse

6 sprigs parsley, chopped coarse

2 medium carrots, chopped coarse

1 teaspoon dried marjoram

½ teaspoon whole peppercorns

¼ cup fresh lemon juice

Combine all ingredients in a large stockpot and bring to a boil. Reduce heat and simmer, uncovered, for 50 minutes. Line a strainer with damp cheesecloth and strain the fish stock into a clean container. Cool at room temperature, then store in the refrigerator for up to two days (or freeze for up to four months).

Makes 2 quarts stock

Nutritional Information per Serving (based on 8 servings)

Calories • 49	Calories from Fat • 14	Percent of Calories from Fat • 28%	Fat • 1.5g
Protein • 7.6g	Carbohydrate • 0.8g	Cholesterol • 0mg	Sodium • 10mg

CHICKEN BROTH

1 4- to 5-pound stewing chicken, cut up and skin removed
6 cups cold water
2 medium carrots, chopped coarse
1 medium green bell pepper, chopped coarse

1 medium onion, chopped coarse
2 celery stalks, with leaves, chopped coarse
1 bay leaf
6 whole peppercorns

Combine all ingredients in a dutch oven. Bring to a boil, cover, and reduce heat. Simmer for 2 hours. Remove chicken. Cool broth using method described on page 3. Skim fat from the surface and discard. Strain broth and refrigerate or freeze.

Makes about 1 quart broth

CHICKEN BROTH

Chicken broth or bouillon is stronger than chicken stock. Stock is made using only bones and vegetables. Broth can be made by reducing stock or by starting with an entire chicken. For a healthier broth, remove all skin from the chicken before cooking, and skim off all the surface fat after the broth is cooked. Use the cooked chicken meat for salads or other dishes that call for cooked chicken.

Nutritional Information per Serving (based on 4 servings)

Calories • 25	Calories from Fat • 8	Percent of Calories from Fat • 30%	Fat • 1g
Protein • 3.4g	Carbohydrate • 0.9g	Cholesterol • 10mg	Sodium • 22mg

BEEF STOCK

4 pounds beef shank bones

3 large onions, quartered

3 medium carrots, chopped coarse

6 cloves garlic, chopped coarse

4 sprigs parsley, chopped coarse

1 teaspoon celery seed

1 teaspoon dried thyme

1 teaspoon dried marjoram

3 bay leaves

½ teaspoon whole peppercorns

1½ cups unsalted tomato juice

10 cups cold water

BAY LEAF

Bay leaf is an herb that should be used sparingly because of its strong flavor. Many southern stews and gumbos use whole bay leaves that are removed before serving. A bay leaf added to a canister of flour will repel mealworms (weevils).

Preheat oven to 400°F. Place bones in a large roasting pan and roast for 30 minutes. Add onion, carrot, and garlic, and roast an additional 30 minutes. Transfer meat and vegetables to a large stockpot. Add remaining ingredients and bring slowly to a boil. (Water should cover by 1 inch.) Reduce heat and simmer for 15 minutes. Cover, leaving the lid slightly ajar for steam to escape, and simmer slowly for at least 8 to 10 hours.

Cool stock at room temperature, then refrigerate, uncovered, overnight.

Skim the fat from the surface of the stock and discard. Reheat stock until it becomes liquid, then strain. Pour into 2- to 4-cup containers, and refrigerate or freeze.

Makes about 10 cups stock

Nutritional Information per Serving (based on 10 servings)

Calories • 152	Calories from Fat • 138	Percent of Calories from Fat • 90%	Fat • 15.3g
Protein • 1.7g	Carbohydrate • 2.3g	Cholesterol • 16mg	Sodium • 88mg

BLACK-EYED PEA SOUP

1½ cups dried black-eyed peas
5 cups cold water
1 medium onion, chopped fine
1 stalk celery, chopped fine
½ teaspoon salt
½ teaspoon freshly ground
   black pepper

1 pound low-fat smoked turkey
   ham
1 5⅓-ounce can (⅔ cup)
   evaporated skim milk
1 tablespoon all-purpose flour

Wash and sort peas, removing all debris, then place in a large stockpot and cover with warm water. Soak for 45 minutes. Drain peas and replace water with 5 cups cold water. Bring to a boil, reduce heat, and then simmer, covered, for 45 minutes. Add onion, celery, salt, pepper, and turkey ham. Simmer over medium heat for 2 hours, stirring occasionally, until peas are tender.

Warm the milk, then combine a small amount with the flour in a small bowl to make a paste. Gradually stir in the remaining milk and continue stirring until well blended. Add flour and milk mixture to soup. Cook and stir until the soup comes to a boil and thickens.

Makes 6—8 servings

BLACK-EYED PEAS

One of the most frequently used legumes in soul food, black-eyed peas came to this country from Africa. Black-eyed peas are often eaten for luck (especially on New Year's Day). Sometimes referred to as "field peas" because they were planted around the edges of fields, black-eyed peas are related to cowpeas.

Nutritional Information per Serving (based on 8 servings)

Calories • 202	Calories from Fat • 29	Percent of Calories from Fat • 14%	Fat • 3.3g
Protein • 20.5g	Carbohydrate • 23.6g	Cholesterol • 51mg	Sodium • 818mg

CRAB SOUP

6 medium carrots, sliced thin

2 medium onions, chopped fine

2 large stalks celery, chopped fine

3 medium potatoes, cut into small cubes

1 cup fresh or frozen corn

1 14½-ounce can tomatoes

3 fresh tomatoes, chopped fine

1 cup shredded cabbage

1 pound turkey ham, cut into small cubes

6 cups Chicken Broth (see Index) or 6 cups water

Cajun Spice Mix (see Index), to taste

1 teaspoon Worcestershire sauce

½ teaspoon dry mustard

2 teaspoons parsley flakes

2 10-ounce packages frozen mixed vegetables

6 1-pound fresh or frozen whole crabs, cleaned and shelled

1 pound fresh or frozen crabmeat

In a large stockpot, combine all the ingredients except frozen vegetables, crabs, and crabmeat. Simmer for 25 minutes.

Add frozen vegetables, crabs, and crabmeat. Simmer an additional 30 minutes.

Makes 6—8 servings

Nutritional Information per Serving (based on 8 servings)

Calories • 327	Calories from Fat • 49	Percent of Calories from Fat • 14%	Fat • 5.4g
Protein • 30.9g	Carbohydrate • 40.3g	Cholesterol • 114mg	Sodium • 968mg

SHRIMP SOUP

Nonstick cooking spray
1 medium onion, chopped fine
2 cloves garlic, minced
8 ounces fresh mushrooms,
   sliced
¼ cup green bell pepper, finely
   chopped
½ cup finely chopped scallion

2 13¾-ounce cans potato soup
2 cups Chicken Broth (see Index)
1½ cups evaporated skim milk
8 ounces scallops
1½ pounds medium fresh shrimp,
   cleaned and deveined
¼ teaspoon cayenne
¼ teaspoon dried thyme

Coat a large skillet with nonstick cooking spray, and heat over medium heat. Sauté onion, garlic, and mushroom until onion is wilted. Add bell pepper and scallion, and sauté an additional 5 minutes. Transfer to a large stockpot. Add remaining ingredients. Bring to a boil, reduce heat and simmer for 15 to 20 minutes.

Makes 6 servings

Nutritional Information per Serving (based on 6 servings)

Calories • 244	Calories from Fat • 27	Percent of Calories from Fat • 11%	Fat • 3g
Protein • 34g	Carbohydrate • 19.5g	Cholesterol • 196mg	Sodium • 969mg

BOUILLABAISSE

Nonstick cooking spray
⅓ cup Cajun Roux (see Index)
1 medium onion, chopped fine
   (1 cup)
6 cloves garlic, minced
2 tablespoons finely chopped
   celery
2 medium tomatoes, chopped
   coarse (1 cup)
3 bay leaves
⅛ teaspoon dried thyme
2 tablespoons finely chopped
   parsley
½ cup dry white wine

2 pounds redfish fillets
1 pound trout fillets
2 quarts cold water
2 teaspoons salt
½ teaspoon freshly ground black
   pepper
⅛ teaspoon cayenne
2 tablespoons fresh lemon juice
6 1-pound fresh or frozen whole
   crabs, cleaned, cooked, and split
   into halves
1 cup crawfish tails (in season)
1 pound medium shrimp, peeled
   and deveined, with tails intact

Coat a heavy, 7- to 10-quart stockpot with nonstick cooking spray. Add roux, onion, garlic, and celery. Cook over low heat, stirring constantly, until vegetables are tender and begin to brown (about 5 minutes).

Stir in tomato, bay leaves, thyme, parsley, wine, ½ pound of the red-fish fillets, and ¼ pound of the trout fillets. Bring to a boil, lower heat, and simmer. Add water, salt, black pepper, cayenne, and lemon juice, and continue to simmer for about 20 minutes.

Add the remaining fish, the crabmeat, and the crawfish, and cook 10 minutes longer. Add the shrimp and cook 5 minutes. Remove and discard bay leaves. Remove pot from heat, and let stand 7 minutes before serving.

Makes 8—10 servings

Nutritional Information per Serving (based on 10 servings)

Calories • 210	Calories from Fat • 28	Percent of Calories from Fat • 14%	Fat • 3.2g
Protein • 37.5g	Carbohydrate • 3.8g	Cholesterol • 195mg	Sodium • 611mg

CHICKEN VEGETABLE SOUP

2 2½-pound stewing chickens, cut up and skin removed

5 quarts cold water

1 tablespoon poultry seasoning

1 teaspoon Cajun Spice Mix (see Index) or seasoning salt (or to taste)

1 28-ounce can whole tomatoes

3 medium white potatoes, peeled and diced fine (3 cups)

3 medium carrots, peeled and chopped fine (2 cups)

5 stalks celery, chopped fine (2½ cups)

2 medium onions, chopped fine

2 green bell peppers, chopped fine

2 chicken bouillon cubes

1 teaspoon dried red pepper flakes

1 cup uncooked elbow macaroni

Place chicken pieces in a stockpot large enough to hold 4 gallons of soup. Add water, poultry seasoning, and Cajun Spice Mix. Bring to a boil, reduce heat, and simmer for 25 minutes.

Add remaining ingredients except macaroni, and simmer 1 hour. Add macaroni and cook 15 minutes, stirring occasionally. Adjust seasoning to taste.

Makes 10 servings

Nutritional Information per Serving (based on 10 servings)

Calories • 189	Calories from Fat • 22	Percent of Calories from Fat • 11%	Fat • 2.4g
Protein • 10.8g	Carbohydrate • 32.5g	Cholesterol • 20mg	Sodium • 395mg

Corn Chowder

9 ears fresh sweet corn

8 cups Chicken Broth (see Index)

2 stalks celery, diced fine (1 cup)

2 medium carrots, diced (1 cup)

1 large white potato, diced (1 cup)

1 medium white onion, chopped fine (1 cup)

Salt and pepper to taste, or Cajun Seasoning Mix (see Index)

1½—2 cups skim milk

8 ounces turkey ham, cut into ½-inch cubes

¼ chopped fresh parsley

Slice corn kernels off cobs into a large stockpot. Scrape the cobs with the back of a knife, removing as much of the remaining kernels and "milk" as possible. Add chicken broth, celery, carrot, potato, and onion to stockpot. Cover, bring slowly to a boil, and reduce heat. Simmer slowly until vegetables are tender, about 25—30 minutes. Season to taste with salt and pepper or Cajun Seasoning Mix. Add milk and heat to serving temperature, but *do not allow to boil*. Garnish each serving with diced turkey and chopped parsley.

Makes 4—6 servings

Nutritional Information per Serving (based on 6 servings)

Calories • 322	Calories from Fat • 40	Percent of Calories from Fat • 11%	Fat • 4.4g
Protein • 20.9g	Carbohydrate • 57.3g	Cholesterol • 48mg	Sodium • 523mg

COUNTRY CHICKEN CHOWDER

2 13¾-ounce cans condensed
   chicken noodle soup
1 pound cooked chicken breast,
   cut into ½-inch cubes (2 cups)
1 medium onion, chopped fine
1 14½-ounce can cream-style
   corn

1 cup cold water
1 5⅓-ounce can (⅔ cup)
   evaporated skim milk
½ teaspoon white pepper
2 tablespoons chopped fresh
   parsley

Skim off fat from top of canned soup with paper towel. Combine soup, chicken, onion, corn, water, milk, and pepper in a large stockpot. Bring to a boil, reduce heat, and simmer 10 minutes. Ladle into serving bowls and sprinkle with parsley.

Makes 8—10 servings

Nutritional Information per Serving (based on 10 servings)

Calories • 166	Calories from Fat • 28	Percent of Calories from Fat • 17%	Fat • 3.1g
Protein • 17.9g	Carbohydrate • 16.9g	Cholesterol • 38mg	Sodium • 758mg

Cajun Catfish Stew

1½ pounds catfish fillets (thick), cut into 1-inch pieces

1 teaspoon Cajun Spice Mix (see Index)

1 teaspoon canola oil

2 medium onions, diced fine

6 cloves garlic, minced fine

2 stalks celery, diced fine

1 large green bell pepper, cut into ¾-inch chunks

6 medium carrots, halved lengthwise, cut into ¼-inch slices

6 large potatoes (1½ pounds), peeled and cut into ½-inch cubes

3 small zucchini, cut into ½-inch slices

1 28-ounce can tomatoes, drained (juice reserved), and cut into ¾-inch chunks

1 teaspoon dried thyme

½ teaspoon dried red pepper flakes

2 cups frozen peas

Wash the catfish and pat dry. Sprinkle generously with half the Cajun Spice Mix and set aside. Heat oil in a large, 5- to 6-quart nonstick saucepan or dutch oven. Add onion and garlic, and sauté for 3 to 5 minutes or until soft. Add celery and bell pepper, and sauté 3 minutes longer. Add carrot, potato, zucchini, tomatoes with their juice, remaining ½ teaspoon Cajun Spice Mix, thyme, and red pepper flakes. Stir to combine, then bring to a boil. Reduce heat, cover, and simmer for 5 minutes. Gently stir in the frozen peas and the catfish. (Make sure the fish is covered with liquid.) Simmer for 10 minutes or until the fish and vegetables are completely cooked.

Makes 10 servings

Nutritional Information per Serving (based on 10 servings)

Calories • 223	Calories from Fat • 27	Percent of Calories from Fat • 12%	Fat • 3g
Protein • 16.5g	Carbohydrate • 34g	Cholesterol • 40mg	Sodium • 234mg

CATFISH STEW

3 cups cold water

4 medium potatoes, diced fine

1 large onion, chopped fine

¼ cup finely chopped red bell
pepper

2 tablespoons finely chopped
garlic

½ small green cabbage, chopped
fine

2 large tomatoes, chopped fine

2 tablespoons Cajun Spice Mix
(see Index)

4 fresh catfish fillets, halved

Combine water, potato, onion, bell pepper, and garlic in a large stock-pot. Cook on high heat 15 minutes. Lower heat. Add cabbage, tomato, and Cajun Spice Mix. Cook 10 minutes, add catfish, and cook 15 minutes more, until fish is flaky but not mushy. Adjust seasoning to taste.

Makes 4—6 servings

Nutritional Information per Serving (based on 6 servings)

Calories • 229	Calories from Fat • 32	Percent of Calories from Fat • 13%	Fat • 3.5g
Protein • 21.6g	Carbohydrate • 28.9g	Cholesterol • 62mg	Sodium • 621mg

Chicken Curry Stew

½ cup all-purpose flour

1 teaspoon salt

⅛ teaspoon freshly ground black pepper

1 2½- to 3-pound broiler-fryer, cut up and skin removed

2 tablespoons margarine

2 tablespoons finely minced onion

2 tablespoons finely chopped parsley

1 clove garlic, crushed

1 14½-ounce can tomatoes

2 teaspoons curry powder

1 teaspoon ground coriander

½ teaspoon dried thyme

¼ cup golden raisins

3 cups cooked long-grain white rice

Combine flour, salt, and pepper, and coat chicken pieces with the mixture. Melt margarine in a large skillet. Add onion, parsley, and garlic, and cook until onion is soft. Add tomatoes, curry powder, coriander, and thyme. Cover and simmer about 40 minutes. Add raisins and simmer 15 minutes longer or until chicken is tender and thoroughly cooked. Serve over hot rice.

Makes 4 servings

Nutritional Information per Serving (based on 4 servings)

Calories • 452	Calories from Fat • 106	Percent of Calories from Fat • 23%	Fat • 11.8g
Protein • 26.5g	Carbohydrate • 59.6g	Cholesterol • 62mg	Sodium • 830mg

CATFISH GUMBO

2 teaspoons canola oil

1 medium onion, chopped fine

4 cloves garlic, minced

2 stalks celery, chopped fine

½ medium green bell pepper, chopped fine

1 16–ounce can diced tomatoes

3 cups Chicken Broth (see Index)

2 bay leaves

½ teaspoon dried thyme

1 teaspoon Cajun Spice Mix (see Index), or to taste

12 ounces fresh okra, trimmed and cut into ½–inch slices

1 cup fresh or frozen corn

1 pound catfish fillets, cut into 1–inch pieces

1½ cups cooked long-grain white rice

Heat oil over low heat in a 4-quart (or larger) saucepan. Add onion, garlic, celery, and bell pepper. Sauté vegetables until tender (about 5 minutes).

Add tomatoes and their juice, chicken broth, bay leaves, thyme, and Cajun Spice Mix. Stir to combine thoroughly, then gently stir in okra. Increase heat to medium–high, and bring the soup to a boil. Reduce heat, cover, and simmer for about 15 minutes. Add corn and catfish; simmer 10 more minutes or until catfish is just cooked through.

Remove bay leaves, and serve gumbo over cooked rice.

Makes 4–5 servings

GUMBO

The word gumbo comes from ngombo, the name Africans gave the okra seeds they hid in their hair during passage across the Atlantic on slave ships. Gumbo is a thick, hearty soup made from whatever local products a cook has on hand. Gumbo, which begins with a roux and is thickened with okra or filé powder, is best when served over hot long-grain white rice.

Nutritional Information per Serving (based on 5 servings)

Calories • 303	Calories from Fat • 89	Percent of Calories from Fat • 28%	Fat • 10g
Protein • 21.2g	Carbohydrate • 34.4g	Cholesterol • 48mg	Sodium • 267mg

CODFISH GUMBO

Nonstick cooking spray

8 ounces fresh okra, trimmed and sliced thin

1 medium onion, sliced thin

2 cloves garlic, minced fine

1 large zucchini, sliced thin

1 28-ounce can tomatoes

2 cups fresh or frozen corn

¼ teaspoon freshly ground black pepper

⅛ teaspoon cayenne

1½ pounds cod steaks

8 cups cooked long-grain white rice

Lightly coat a nonstick skillet with nonstick cooking spray. Add okra, and sauté over medium heat 3 minutes. Add onion and garlic, and sauté 5 minutes longer. Add zucchini and tomatoes with their juice, and cook over low heat 5 minutes. Add corn, black pepper, and cayenne. Place the cod steaks on top of the vegetable mixture, and spoon some of the mixture over them. Cook gently 10 to 12 minutes or until the fish is flaky but not mushy. Serve over hot rice.

Makes 6—8 servings

Nutritional Information per Serving (based on 8 servings)

Calories • 349	Calories from Fat • 13	Percent of Calories from Fat • 4%	Fat • 1.4g
Protein • 22.6g	Carbohydrate • 61.8g	Cholesterol • 37mg	Sodium • 219mg

SEAFOOD GUMBO

2 quarts Chicken Broth (see Index)

1 cup (8 ounces) chopped smoked turkey

2 bay leaves

2 tablespoons dried red pepper flakes

2 teaspoons salt

Nonstick cooking spray

3 cups finely chopped fresh okra

1 medium green bell pepper, minced

2 large onions, chopped fine

2 stalks celery, chopped fine

2 cloves garlic, minced

1 16-ounce can whole tomatoes

⅓ cup Cajun Roux (see Index)

1 tablespoon Tabasco

½ teaspoon dried thyme

1 pound shrimp, deveined

1 6-ounce can crabmeat

1 tablespoon filé powder

10 cups cooked long-grain white rice

Combine chicken broth, turkey, bay leaves, red pepper flakes, and 1 teaspoon of the salt in a large pot. Bring to a boil over high heat. Reduce heat to low, cover, and simmer for 1 hour (stirring every 20 minutes or so).

Spray a large skillet with nonstick cooking spray, and heat over medium heat. Add okra, bell pepper, onion, celery, and garlic. Sauté about 10 minutes, until almost tender. Add tomatoes with their juice and cook 5 minutes longer.

Place sautéed vegetables and roux in hot chicken broth. Stir in remaining 1 teaspoon of salt, Tabasco, and thyme. Reduce heat to low, cover, and simmer for 1 hour.

Stir in shrimp and crabmeat and cook 10 minutes. Add filé powder and cook 10 minutes more. Adjust seasonings to taste and serve over rice.

Makes 10—12 servings

Nutritional Information per Serving (based on 12 servings)

Calories • 328	Calories from Fat • 64	Percent of Calories from Fat • 20%	Fat • 7.1g
Protein • 19.3g	Carbohydrate • 45.5g	Cholesterol • 78mg	Sodium • 756mg

Quick Gumbo

1½ cups Chicken Broth (see Index)
1 14½-ounce can diced tomatoes
3 cups cold water
1 bay leaf
1 tablespoon dried thyme
1 medium onion, chopped fine
¾ cup finely chopped green bell pepper
1 tablespoon minced parsley
1 pound chicken breast, cut into ½-inch cubes (4 cups)
1 teaspoon garlic powder
2 cups frozen whole okra
1 tablespoon filé powder
3 cups cooked long-grain white rice
2 cups frozen baby shrimp, cooked
Salt and freshly ground black pepper
Tabasco

FILÉ POWDER

Filé powder is made from dried and ground sassafras leaves and is used for thickening and flavoring dishes, particularly gumbos and stews. Filé powder must be stirred into a hot sauce just before serving. Never allow filé to boil.

In a large stockpot or dutch oven, combine chicken broth, tomatoes with this juice, water, bay leaf, thyme, onion, bell pepper, parsley, chicken, and garlic powder. Bring to a boil. Reduce heat and simmer 30 minutes.

Add okra and cook according to time on package. Remove from heat and stir in filé powder, rice, and shrimp. Let stand 10 minutes. Remove bay leaf. Season to taste with salt and pepper and Tabasco.

Makes 6—8 servings

Nutritional Information per Serving (based on 8 servings)

Calories • 384	Calories from Fat • 24	Percent of Calories from Fat • 6%	Fat • 2.6g
Protein • 24.5g	Carbohydrate • 63.9g	Cholesterol • 80mg	Sodium • 177mg

SOUTHERN OKRA AND CRAB GUMBO

Nonstick cooking spray
1 stalk celery, chopped fine
2 cloves garlic, minced fine
1 medium onion, chopped fine
½ green bell pepper, chopped fine
3 14½-ounce cans stewed tomatoes
3 cups thinly sliced fresh okra

2 cups unsalted tomato juice
2 bay leaves
1 tablespoon Salt-Free Cajun Seasoning Blend (see Index)
1 pound fresh lump crabmeat, drained and flaked
5 cups cooked long-grain white rice

Lightly coat a large dutch oven with nonstick cooking spray and heat over medium heat. Add celery, garlic, onion, and bell pepper. Sauté until tender (about 5 minutes). Stir in tomatoes with their juice, okra, tomato juice, bay leaves, and Salt-Free Cajun Seasoning Blend. Bring to a boil, reduce heat, and simmer, covered, for 1 hour, stirring occasionally. Stir in crabmeat and cook over low heat until heated (about 5 minutes). Remove and discard bay leaves. Serve hot over rice.

Makes 10 servings

Nutritional Information per Serving (based on 10 servings)

Calories • 201	Calories from Fat • 11	Percent of Calories from Fat • 5%	Fat • 1.2g
Protein • 12.2g	Carbohydrate • 36.5g	Cholesterol • 38mg	Sodium • 486mg

BONNIE'S SOUTHERN CHILI

1 teaspoon canola oil

2 pounds ground turkey

1 large onion, chopped fine

2 cloves garlic, crushed

1 large green bell pepper, cut into
½-inch cubes

1 14½-ounce can stewed tomatoes

1 8-ounce can tomato sauce

1 6-ounce can tomato paste

¼ cup firmly packed dark brown
sugar

1 hot cherry pepper, sliced thin

2 tablespoons chili powder (or to
taste)

2 bay leaves

¼ teaspoon cayenne

2 16-ounce cans red beans or
kidney beans

2 teaspoons Cajun Spice Mix (see
Index), or to taste

Coat a large stockpot evenly with the oil, and heat over medium heat. Add ground turkey, and cook 15 minutes, stirring occasionally. Add onion, garlic, and bell pepper, and cook until tender. Stir in tomatoes with their juice, tomato sauce, tomato paste, brown sugar, cherry pepper, chili powder, bay leaves, cayenne, and beans. Season with Cajun Spice Mix to taste. Stir well, and cook over low heat for 45 minutes. Remove and discard bay leaves before serving.

Makes 10 servings

Nutritional Information per Serving (based on 10 servings)

Calories • 303	Calories from Fat • 97	Percent of Calories from Fat • 29%	Fat • 10.8g
Protein • 25.2g	Carbohydrate • 33g	Cholesterol • 46mg	Sodium • 657mg

2
SALADS

Southern Morning Fruit Salad

Okra Salad

Potato Salad

Crabmeat Salad

Creole Salad

Turkey and Green Bean Cajun Salad

SOUTHERN MORNING FRUIT SALAD

¼ cantaloupe, cut into ½-inch cubes

¼ honeydew melon, cut into ½-inch cubes

¼ fresh pineapple, cut into ½-inch cubes

2 peaches, peeled, pitted, and sliced lengthwise

8 ounces whole grapes

2 oranges, peeled, sectioned, and seeded

2 bananas, cut into 1-inch-thick slices

Sauce

1 16-ounce carton fat-free sour cream

¼ cup firmly packed brown sugar

2 tablespoons honey

Juice of 1 orange

Juice of ½ lemon

3 tablespoons pineapple juice

½ teaspoon cinnamon

¼ teaspoon nutmeg

Combine all the fruit except bananas in a large bowl. Refrigerate 2 hours.

Chill appropriate number of salad dishes. In a medium bowl, combine the ingredients for the sauce. Chill 1 hour. To serve, add bananas to fruit mixture. Spoon into individual chilled dishes, and top with sauce.

Makes 8—10 servings

Nutritional Information per Serving (based on 10 servings)

Calories • 148	Calories from Fat • 4	Percent of Calories from Fat • 2%	Fat • 0.5g
Protein • 4.3g	Carbohydrate • 35.2g	Cholesterol • 0mg	Sodium • 42mg

OKRA SALAD

8 ounces small fresh okra pods, tops and tails removed

1 teaspoon Cajun Spice Mix (see Index), or to taste

4 cups torn iceberg lettuce

2 cups washed and torn fresh spinach

6 scallions, with tops, minced

2 cloves garlic, crushed

⅔ cup bottled fat-free vinaigrette dressing

OKRA

The word okra comes from okruma, the word for "vegetable" in Ghana. Okra was brought to the southern United States on slave ships. Africans carried its seed (which they called ngomba) hidden in their hair. Okra is very popular in Creole cooking. The pods are used as a thickener for soups, stews, gumbos, and sauces. When purchasing fresh okra, look for small pods with even color.

Wash okra. Blanch in a medium saucepan with Cajun Spice Mix. Drain, and refrigerate for 2 hours. In a large salad bowl, combine lettuce, spinach, okra, scallion, garlic, and dressing. Toss and serve.

Makes 5 servings

Nutritional Information per Serving (based on 5 servings)

Calories • 37	Calories from Fat • 3	Percent of Calories from Fat • 5%	Fat • 0.3g
Protein • 2.2g	Carbohydrate • 8.1g	Cholesterol • 0mg	Sodium • 533mg

POTATO SALAD

6 large Idaho potatoes, scrubbed
1 stalk celery, diced fine
½ medium onion, chopped fine
6 hard–boiled eggs (discard 5 yolks)
½ teaspoon garlic powder

⅛ teaspoon cayenne
Salt and freshly ground pepper to taste
1 tablespoon prepared mustard
3 tablespoons sweet pickle relish
½ cup fat–free sour cream

Boil unpeeled potatoes until soft, about 45 minutes. Cool, peel, and dice fine. In a large bowl, combine potatoes, celery, onion, eggs, garlic powder, cayenne, salt, and pepper. In a separate bowl, combine mustard, relish, and sour cream. Toss dressing with salad, and chill for at least 1 hour before serving.

Makes 8 servings

Nutritional Information per Serving (based on 8 servings)

Calories • 122	Calories from Fat • 2.2	Percent of Calories from Fat • 2%	Fat • 0.3g
Protein • 5.7g	Carbohydrate • 25.2g	Cholesterol • 0mg	Sodium • 131mg

Crabmeat Salad

8 ounces frozen crabmeat, thawed and drained

½ large cucumber, peeled, seeded, and diced

1 stalk celery, diced

¼ cup finely diced red onion

¼ cup finely chopped scallion

2 tablespoons finely chopped fresh parsley

1 tablespoon minced fresh dill

4 tablespoons nonfat plain yogurt

1 teaspoon Cajun Spice Mix (see Index)

4 romaine lettuce leaves

2 medium tomatoes, cut into 4 wedges each

1 teaspoon fresh lemon juice

Chill four salad plates. In a large mixing bowl, combine crabmeat, cucumber, celery, onion, scallion, parsley, dill, yogurt, and Cajun Spice Mix. Mix well. Cover with plastic wrap, and refrigerate at least 1 hour. To serve, line chilled salad plates with lettuce leaves and top each with one–fourth of the crab mixture. Arrange tomato wedges around the crab mixture, and sprinkle each salad with lemon juice.

Makes 4 servings

Nutritional Information per Serving (based on 4 servings)

Calories • 85	Calories from Fat • 11	Percent of Calories from Fat • 13%	Fat • 1.3g
Protein • 11.8g	Carbohydrate • 7.2g	Cholesterol • 48mg	Sodium • 209mg

CREOLE SALAD

1 head iceberg lettuce torn into bite-sized pieces

3 medium cucumbers, peeled, seeded, and cut into small cubes

1 dozen small pickled onions

1/4 cup raisins

1 medium apple, cored and cut into 1/2-inch cubes

1/2 large green bell pepper, cut into 1-inch squares

1/4 cup bottled fat-free French or Catalina dressing

In a large bowl, combine all ingredients except dressing. Refrigerate at least 1 hour. Before serving, toss with dressing.

Makes 6 servings

Nutritional Information per Serving (based on 6 servings)

Calories • 81	Calories from Fat • 5	Percent of Calories from Fat • 5%	Fat • 0.6g
Protein • 2.4g	Carbohydrate • 18.1g	Cholesterol • 0mg	Sodium • 234mg

Turkey and Green Bean Cajun Salad

1 pound cooked turkey breast, cut into ¾-inch cubes (3 cups)

1 pound cooked fresh green beans, cut into 1-inch pieces (3 cups)

1 cup nonfat plain yogurt

¼ cup finely chopped fresh parsley

⅓ cup fresh lemon juice

2 tablespoons frozen apple juice concentrate, thawed

1 medium red apple, cored and diced fine

¼ cup raisins

¾ teaspoon Cajun Spice Mix (see Index)

3 cups chopped iceberg lettuce

Chill six salad plates. Combine all ingredients except lettuce in a large bowl. Cover and refrigerate at least 1 hour. Line chilled salad plates with lettuce, and spoon one-sixth of the salad mixture onto each plate.

Makes 6 servings

Nutritional Information per Serving (based on 6 servings)

Calories • 199	Calories from Fat • 10	Percent of Calories from Fat • 5%	Fat • 1.1g
Protein • 27g	Carbohydrate • 21.7g	Cholesterol • 64mg	Sodium • 100mg

3

BEANS, BEANS, AND MORE BEANS

Mississippi Beans

Old-Fashioned Baked Lima Beans

White Beans with Sage

Black-Eyed Peas and Rice

Butter Beans and Rice

Red Beans and Rice

Black-Eyed Pea Jambalaya

White Beans with Turkey

Pinto Beans with Turkey Ham

Dried beans and peas provide fiber like no other foods. Beans and peas can be used as vegetables, or they can (and should) be frequently substituted for meats to reduce daily fat consumption.

Beans are available dried, canned, or frozen. Once cooked, they can be stored in the refrigerator for up to three days or frozen for longer periods. Beans and peas can be used in salads and soups, as side dishes, or in dips. They can also be used in casseroles, one-pot meals, or stews.

Perhaps the most common bean dish in African American cooking is Red Beans and Rice. Red beans were traditionally cooked on wash day. As the wash dried on the line, the beans cooked for many hours. As one of 12 children, I can remember eating beans three or four times a week. Beans were inexpensive and went a long way when served over rice.

Today's health-wise cooks prepare bean dishes not with the pig tails and backbones of yesteryear, but with healthier meats that keep our traditions alive without excessive fats. Low-fat and fat-free smoked turkey, for example, provide a new way of introducing these meals to future generations.

MISSISSIPPI BEANS

8 ounces smoked turkey, cut into
   ½–inch cubes (1 cup)

2 pounds green beans, cut in half

2 medium onions, quartered

1 teaspoon salt

1 teaspoon sugar

¼ teaspoon cayenne

1 pound new potatoes, peeled

Place turkey cubes in a large saucepan. Cover with water and boil 15 minutes. Add green beans, onion, salt, sugar, and cayenne. Boil 15 minutes. Add potatoes, and continue to boil until potatoes are tender (about 20 minutes).

Makes 6 servings

Nutritional Information per Serving (based on 6 servings)

Calories • 225	Calories from Fat • 56	Percent of Calories from Fat • 25%	Fat • 6.6g
Protein • 11.2g	Carbohydrate • 33.6g	Cholesterol • 0mg	Sodium • 773mg

OLD-FASHIONED BAKED LIMA BEANS

3 cups large dried lima beans
2 quarts cold water
1 medium onion, chopped
1 bay leaf
2 stalks celery, chopped
¼ cup chopped fresh parsley

⅓ cup light molasses
¼ cup firmly packed brown
  sugar
2 teaspoons dry mustard
1¼ teaspoons salt

In a large saucepan, cover beans with water and soak overnight. Drain and rinse thoroughly. Add the 2 quarts of cold water, and boil until beans begin to soften. Drain off water until the beans are just covered, then transfer to a shallow baking dish. Preheat oven to 325°F. In a medium bowl, combine remaining ingredients. Pour over beans. Cover and bake for 1½ to 2 hours or until sauce bubbles.

Makes 6—8 servings

Nutritional Information per Serving (based on 8 servings)

Calories • 298	Calories from Fat • 7	Percent of Calories from Fat • 2%	Fat • 0.8g
Protein • 14.9g	Carbohydrate • 60g	Cholesterol • 0mg	Sodium • 367mg

White Beans with Sage

2 cups cooked Great Northern
  beans (or 2 14½-ounce cans,
  drained)
8 ounces turkey ham (or cooked
  turkey thighs), cut into 1-inch
  cubes (1 cup)
1 medium tomato, chopped fine
½ medium onion, chopped fine
½ medium yellow bell pepper,
  cut into 1-inch squares

1 teaspoon dried sage
1 teaspoon vegetable oil
½ teaspoon salt
¼ teaspoon freshly ground black
1 clove garlic, chopped fine

Cook dried beans as directed on package. (Do not use salt.) Drain. (It is not necessary to cook canned beans.) In a 2-quart saucepan cook remaining ingredients over medium heat for 10 minutes, stirring occasionally, until onions is tender. Stir in beans, and cook 10 more minutes.

Makes 6 servings

Nutritional Information per Serving (based on 6 servings)

Calories • 141	Calories from Fat • 28	Percent of Calories from Fat • 20%	Fat • 3.1g
Protein • 12.7g	Carbohydrate • 16g	Cholesterol • 22mg	Sodium • 559mg

BLACK-EYED PEAS AND RICE

2 pounds dried black-eyed peas

3 quarts cold water

1 medium onion, chopped fine

½ medium green bell pepper, chopped fine

¼ cup finely chopped celery

2 tablespoons finely minced fresh parsley

2 pounds turkey ham, cut into 1-inch cubes

1 teaspoon salt

¾ teaspoon freshly ground black pepper

⅛ teaspoon cayenne

3 bay leaves

½ teaspoon dried thyme

½ teaspoon dried basil

8 cups cooked long-grain white rice

Sort and rinse peas, then soak in a large saucepan or dutch oven overnight. Drain. Cover rinsed beans with 3 quarts of cold water. Add remaining ingredients except rice, and simmer, covered, about 1½ to 2 hours, until the peas are tender but not mushy and a natural gravy has formed. Add additional water as needed to keep peas covered throughout cooking. Serve over cooked rice.

Makes 8—10 servings

Nutritional Information per Serving (based on 10 servings)

Calories • 554	Calories from Fat • 55	Percent of Calories from Fat • 10%	Fat • 6.1g
Protein • 29.5g	Carbohydrate • 93.3g	Cholesterol • 51mg	Sodium • 1,132mg

BUTTER BEANS AND RICE

2 pounds dried butter beans
  (small limas)
1 cup finely chopped onion
1 tablespoon finely minced garlic
1½ pounds turkey ham, cut into
  ½-inch cubes
1 teaspoon Cajun Spice Mix (see
  Index)

2 bay leaves
⅛ teaspoon ground mace
2½ quarts cold water
8 cups cooked long-grain white
  rice

Soak beans overnight in cold water at least twice the depth of the beans. Drain off the water, and combine the beans with remaining ingredients, except water and rice, in a heavy, 8- to 10-quart pot. Add cold water to just cover. Bring to a boil, reduce heat, and simmer for 1½ to 2 hours, until beans are tender but not mushy. Stir frequently during cooking, scraping the sides and bottom of the pot with a wooden spoon to prevent scorching.

When beans are finished cooking, remove from heat and let stand at room temperature for 1½ hours. Remove and discard bay leaves. Do not reheat beans; heat individual servings as needed in a separate saucepan, and freeze remaining beans in individual containers for reheating later. If beans dry out, add a small amount of water.

Serve over cooked rice.

Makes 8—10 servings

Nutritional Information per Serving (based on 10 servings)

Calories • 565	Calories from Fat • 43	Percent of Calories from Fat • 8%	Fat • 4.8g
Protein • 35.3g	Carbohydrate • 95g	Cholesterol • 38mg	Sodium • 717mg

RED BEANS AND RICE

1 pound dried kidney beans
8—10 cups cold water
Nonstick cooking spray
1 large onion, chopped fine
½ medium green bell pepper, chopped fine
¼ cup finely chopped celery
3 cloves garlic, minced
1 pound turkey ham (or turkey thigh meat), cut into 1-inch cubes

2 tablespoons finely chopped parsley
⅛ teaspoon dried red pepper flakes
½ teaspoon Cajun Spice Mix (see Index)
2 bay leaves
5 cups cooked long-grain white rice

Soak beans 8 hours or overnight. Drain and transfer to a stockpot. Add cold water to cover.

Coat a large skillet with nonstick cooking spray and heat over medium heat. Add onion, bell pepper, celery, and garlic, and sauté until tender. Add sautéed mixture to beans along with turkey ham, parsley, red pepper flakes, Cajun Spice Mix, and bay leaves. Bring to a boil, lower heat, and simmer, stirring occasionally, for 2 to 3 hours, until beans are tender and a thick gravy has formed. If beans seem too dry, add about 1 cup of water toward the end of cooking. Before serving, remove and discard bay leaves. Serve over hot rice.

RED BEANS

The key to perfect red beans is to use a heavy pot and very low heat—just hot enough to prevent the beans from sticking during cooking. Remember: Extra water can always be added toward the end of cooking just before serving.

Makes 8—10 servings

Nutritional Information per Serving (based on 10 servings)

Calories • 324	Calories from Fat • 27	Percent of Calories from Fat • 8%	Fat • 3g
Protein • 21.8g	Carbohydrate • 52.2g	Cholesterol • 25mg	Sodium • 483mg

Black-Eyed Pea Jambalaya

1¼ cups dried black-eyed peas, sorted and rinsed

5 cups cold water

1 medium onion, chopped fine

½ cup chopped scallion

½ medium green bell pepper, chopped fine (½ cup)

¼ cup chopped fresh parsley

2 cloves garlic, crushed

1 14½-ounce can diced tomatoes

1 cup turkey ham, cut into 1-inch cubes

½ teaspoon cayenne

¼ teaspoon salt

⅛ teaspoon dried oregano

⅛ teaspoon dried thyme

1 bay leaf

1 cup long-grain white rice, uncooked

JAMBALAYA

Jambalaya is a stew first introduced in Louisiana when the Spaniards took over New Orleans in the late eighteenth century. Jambalaya can be made with ham, sausages, or seafood, but the main ingredient is always rice.

Place peas in a large saucepan or dutch oven. Add enough cold water to cover by 2 inches, and soak overnight

Drain peas and return to pan. Add 5 cups of fresh cold water to cover peas. Bring to a boil, reduce heat, and simmer, covered, for 45 minutes. Add remaining ingredients except rice, and simmer 45 minutes longer. Stir in rice, cover, and simmer 20 more minutes or until peas and rice are tender. Remove and discard bay leaf before serving.

Makes 6 servings

Nutritional Information per Serving (based on 6 servings)

Calories • 268	Calories from Fat • 17	Percent of Calories from Fat • 6%	Fat • 1.9g
Protein • 10.4g	Carbohydrate • 52.4g	Cholesterol • 11mg	Sodium • 404mg

WHITE BEANS WITH TURKEY

2 pounds dried white beans

3 quarts cold water

½ medium green bell pepper, chopped fine (½ cup)

½ cup thinly sliced scallion tops

6 cloves garlic, minced fine

1½ pounds smoked turkey thighs, cut into 1-inch pieces

2 bay leaves

1½ teaspoons Cajun Spice Mix (see Index)

1 cup turkey sausage, sliced into 1-inch cubes

8 cups cooked long-grain white rice

Soak beans overnight. Drain beans and transfer them to a heavy 8- to 10-quart pot. Add remaining ingredients except sausage and rice, and bring to a boil. Lower heat and simmer for 1½ hours. Add sausage and cook 1 hour longer, until beans are tender. During cooking, stir the sides and bottom of the pot to prevent scorching, and add additional water if the mixture appears dry.

Remove and discard bay leaves. Serve over rice.

Makes 8—10 servings

Nutritional Information per Serving (based on 10 servings)

Calories • 651	Calories from Fat • 115	Percent of Calories from Fat • 17%	Fat • 12.7g
Protein • 38.5g	Carbohydrate • 96.5g	Cholesterol • 8mg	Sodium • 882mg

Pinto Beans with Turkey Ham

1 pound dried pinto beans
8 ounces turkey ham, cut into
   ½-inch cubes (1 cup)
1 medium onion, chopped fine
1 bay leaf

2 teaspoons Cajun Spice Mix (see
   Index)
8 cups cooked long-grain white
   rice

In a medium saucepan, soak beans overnight in enough cold water to cover by 4 inches. Drain beans and return to saucepan. Add fresh water to cover, turkey ham, onion, bay leaf, and Cajun Spice Mix. Bring to a boil, reduce heat, and simmer 2 hours or until beans are tender. (Add water during cooking if beans appear dry.)

Remove and discard bay leaf. Serve over rice.

Makes 8—10 servings

Nutritional Information per Serving (based on 10 servings)

Calories • 355	Calories from Fat • 19	Percent of Calories from Fat • 5%	Fat • 2.1g
Protein • 17.4g	Carbohydrate • 65.8g	Cholesterol • 13mg	Sodium • 241mg

4

MAIN COURSES

Catfish Étouffée

Burned Fish

Oven-Fried Catfish

Creole Catfish Bake

Oven-Fried Trout

Cajun-Style Haddock

Seasoned Crab Cakes

Louisiana Shrimp Creole

Shrimp Étouffée

Shrimp Sauté

Shrimp-Stuffed Peppers

Quick and Spicy Shrimp

Shrimp Curry

Smothered Chicken

Oven-Fried Chicken

Chicken and Dumplings

French Quarter Chicken Breasts

Cajun Chicken and "Dirty" Rice

Country Chicken

Chicken and Kidney Beans

Pepper Chicken

Chicken Curry

Turkey-Stuffed Bell Peppers

Turkey Wings and Gravy

Turkey and Peppers

Turkey Breakfast Sausage

African American cooking includes a variety of seafood dishes. From the bayou to the Garden District, fish is the Friday meal in New Orleans.

FISH TIPS

- An average-size serving of fish is 6 to 8 ounces.
- Eyes should be clear and protruding from the sockets, not clouded and sunken.
- Flesh should be firm to the touch, never mushy or slimy.
- Fresh fish should never be dry.
- Gills should be bright red.
- Never cook fish to an internal temperature of more than 130°F. No matter the cooking method, remember that fish is very delicate.
- Test for doneness by checking if fish flakes easily with a fork.
- Remember that shellfish are higher in cholesterol than fin fish.

SHRIMP

When I was growing up in New Orleans, shrimp was plentiful and cheap. The task of cleaning became a time to gather all my sisters together and race to see who could clean the most. Our family meals included a wide variety of dishes using shrimp: everything from gumbo to scrambled eggs with shrimp and hot sauce. But the best way to cook shrimp was to simply boil whole shrimp in a spicy court bouillon or with some Louisiana shrimp boil. We shelled them on newspapers and ate them with our fingers at the kitchen table or on the front porch with neighbors.

POULTRY

When I was growing up, we had chicken every Sunday—a real specialty because we rarely had meat enough to feed our large family. During the week, Mama would use less expensive meat products to "stretch" the meals. On Sunday, it was a treat to have your own chicken thigh or leg.

Visiting my grandmother in Mississippi, we had to catch and pre- pare a bird for the evening meal. My job was to help my grandmother pluck and singe the feathers. I hated this task, but when the chickens were prepared (usually sautéed or fried), I thoroughly enjoyed the out- come.

To reduce the amount of fat in meals, the recipes in this book *always* require removal of the chicken or turkey skin and all visible fat.

Guidelines for Storing Chicken

In the Refrigerator
Raw meat. Keep no longer than two days. Cover loosely with plastic wrap to eliminate drying.
Cooked meat. Keep covered for up to five days.

In the Freezer
Raw meat. Keep in a tightly wrapped, airtight container up to two months.
Cooked meat. Keep up to two weeks in an airtight container, plastic wrap, or freezer paper.

In the Deep Freeze
Raw meat. Keep up to six months in an airtight container or freezer paper.
Cooked meat. Keep up to one month in an airtight container.
Thawing frozen chicken. Once you thaw a frozen chicken, *do not refreeze it*. Use it within two days of thawing. Allow 3 to 4 hours of thawing time per pound if the meat is defrosted in the refrigerator. If you are in a rush, you can use the quick method of defrosting: Place a wrapped chicken in a pan under cold running water and allow 30 minutes per pound.
Handling raw chicken. Raw chicken may contain bacteria that can

lead to serious illnesses. Always take extra care to avoid contaminating work surfaces, other foods, and family members.

- Thoroughly wash your hands and any items used while preparing meal.
- Cook chicken to 170°F. (Juices should run clear, and no red or pink flesh should be visible when meat is pulled away from the bone.)
- To disinfect work surfaces, use one part bleach to two parts water.

CATFISH ÉTOUFFÉE

5 tablespoons Cajun Roux (see Index)

2 medium white onions, chopped fine (2 cups)

1 stalk celery, chopped fine (½ cup)

½ medium green bell pepper, chopped fine (½ cup)

3 cloves garlic, chopped fine

3 cups Chicken Broth (see Index)

1 teaspoon Tabasco

1 14-ounce can tomatoes, drained (juice reserved), coarsely chopped

1 teaspoon fresh lemon juice

1 tablespoon Worcestershire sauce

1 bay leaf

1 teaspoon Kitchen Bouquet sauce

¼ teaspoon cayenne

1 cup finely chopped scallion

½ cup finely chopped parsley

2½ pounds catfish fillets, skinned and cut into 1-inch chunks

Salt

6 cups cooked long-grain white rice

In a 5-quart dutch oven, heat roux over low heat, stirring constantly. Add onion, celery, bell pepper, and garlic, and cook, continuing to stir, until vegetables are tender but not brown. Add chicken broth, Tabasco, tomato and their juice, lemon juice, Worcestershire sauce, bay leaf, Kitchen Bouquet sauce, and cayenne. Simmer 1 hour.

Stir in scallion, parsley, and catfish. Cook 15 minutes or until fish is flaky but not mushy. Salt to taste. Serve hot over rice.

Makes 6—8 servings

Nutritional Information per Serving (based on 8 servings)

Calories • 450	Calories from Fat • 138	Percent of Calories from Fat • 31%	Fat • 15.3g
Protein • 28.8g	Carbohydrate • 47.7g	Cholesterol • 70mg	Sodium • 225mg

BURNED FISH

1 teaspoon garlic powder

1 teaspoon lemon pepper

1 teaspoon freshly ground black pepper

1 teaspoon dried rosemary

½ teaspoon dried oregano

1 teaspoon dried basil

4 trout or catfish fillets

Nonstick cooking spray

1½ tablespoons vegetable oil

Combine garlic powder, lemon pepper, black pepper, rosemary, oregano, and basil in a jar and shake to mix well. Rub mixture into each fillet. Lightly coat a large, heavy skillet with cooking spray, add oil, and heat to smoking. Place fillets in skillet, leaving a small space between them. Brown well on both sides ("burn"), and serve immediately.

Makes 4 servings

Nutritional Information per Serving (based on 4 servings)

Calories • 150	Calories from Fat • 75	Percent of Calories from Fat • 50%	Fat • 8.4g
Protein • 16.7g	Carbohydrate • 1.7g	Cholesterol • 46mg	Sodium • 23mg

OVEN-FRIED CATFISH

3 pounds catfish
Nonstick cooking spray
¼ cup fine yellow cornmeal

2 tablespoons Louisiana
  Seasoning Mix (see Index)
4 egg whites (or ½ cup
  cholesterol–free egg substitute)
1 cup nonfat plain yogurt

CATFISH

Southern eating wouldn't be the same without the delectable presence of this scavenger fish. Catfish is traditionally deep-fried, but oven-fried catfish retains the deep-fried taste without all the excess fat.

Preheat oven to 350°F. Wash fish thoroughly and cut into pieces. Coat a heavy baking pan with cooking spray, and heat over medium heat. In a small bowl, combine cornmeal and Louisiana Seasoning Mix. Transfer to a large plate and set aside. In another bowl, beat egg whites and blend with yogurt.

Dip fish into egg mixture, then coat on both sides with cornmeal mixture. Arrange fish on baking pan, and spray top of each piece with cooking spray. Bake 12 minutes, turn, and bake an additional 12 minutes. Thoroughly cooked fish should be flaky, not mushy.

Makes 8 servings

Nutritional Information per Serving (based on 8 servings)

Calories • 271	Calories from Fat • 119	Percent of Calories from Fat • 45%	Fat • 13.2g
Protein • 30.3g	Carbohydrate • 6mg	Cholesterol • 80mg	Sodium • 141mg

CREOLE CATFISH BAKE

Nonstick cooking spray

½ teaspoon brown sugar

½ teaspoon dried basil

½ teaspoon freshly ground black
pepper

4 catfish fillets (about 1 pound),
washed

1 tablespoon vegetable oil

¼ cup minced onion

¼ cup minced red bell pepper

¼ cup minced green bell pepper

6 medium shrimp, cleaned,
deveined, and halved

2 tablespoons tomato paste

½ cup cold water

Salt and black pepper

Preheat oven to 350°F. Coat a large baking pan with cooking spray. Mix brown sugar, basil, and black pepper in a small bowl, and rub into fish fillets. (Reserve fish drippings.) Arrange fillets on the baking pan and sprinkle with oil. Bake 20 minutes.

Coat a small skillet with cooking spray and heat over medium heat. Pour fish drippings into skillet, and sauté onion, red and green pepper, and shrimp for 10 minutes. Add tomato paste and water, and simmer until sauce is reduced by half. Season sauce to taste and serve over hot fish fillets.

Makes 4 servings

Nutritional Information per Serving (based on 4 servings)

Calories • 214	Calories from Fat • 111	Percent of Calories from Fat • 52%	Fat • 12.3g
Protein • 20.2g	Carbohydrate • 5.3g	Cholesterol • 69mg	Sodium • 145mg

Oven-Fried Trout

1 pound trout fillets

3 egg whites, beaten

½ cup 1% low-fat milk

½ cup fine yellow cornmeal

½ teaspoon Cajun Spice Mix (see Index)

Nonstick cooking spray

1 tablespoon vegetable oil

4 lemon wedges

4 sprigs fresh parsley

Preheat oven to 425°F. Rinse fillets under cold water and pat dry. In a medium bowl, beat together egg whites and milk. Set aside. In another bowl, combine cornmeal and Cajun Spice Mix. Coat a large baking dish with cooking spray. Dip fillets first in egg mixture, then in cornmeal mixture, and arrange in a single layer in the baking dish. Brush the top of each fillet with oil.

Bake, uncovered, for 10 minutes on each side, until fish flakes easily when tested with a fork. Serve garnished with lemon wedges and parsley.

Makes 4 servings

Nutritional Information per Serving (based on 4 servings)

Calories • 246	Calories from Fat • 73	Percent of Calories from Fat • 30%	Fat • 8.1g
Protein • 28.3g	Carbohydrate • 13.4g	Cholesterol • 66mg	Sodium • 115mg

CAJUN-STYLE HADDOCK

1 14½-ounce can stewed tomatoes
2 medium stalks celery, chopped
  fine
1 medium onion, chopped fine
½ medium green bell pepper,
  chopped fine
2 cloves garlic, minced

2 bay leaves
¾ teaspoon dried thyme
½ teaspoon Cajun Spice Mix (see
  Index)
1½ pounds haddock fillets
Nonstick cooking spray

Preheat oven to 400°F. In a medium saucepan, combine tomatoes, celery, onion, bell pepper, garlic, bay leaves, thyme, and Cajun Spice Mix. Bring to a boil. Cover, reduce heat, and simmer for 20 minutes, stirring occasionally.

Rinse fillets under cold water and pat dry. Coat a large baking dish with cooking spray. Arrange fillets in baking dish and bake, uncovered, for 15 minutes, until fish flakes easily when tested with a fork. Pour the sauce over the fish. Remove bay leaves from pan before serving.

Makes 6 servings

Nutritional Information per Serving (based on 6 servings)

Calories • 133	Calories from Fat • 9	Percent of Calories from Fat • 7%	Fat • 1g
Protein • 22.6g	Carbohydrate • 8.2g	Cholesterol • 65mg	Sodium • 279mg

Seasoned Crab Cakes

1 pound fresh crabmeat, drained
  and flaked
½ cup dry seasoned breadcrumbs
¼ cup finely chopped white
  onion
2 teaspoons finely chopped fresh
  parsley
2 teaspoons fat-free mayonnaise

1½ teaspoons Worcestershire
  sauce
3 egg whites, beaten
½ teaspoon dry mustard
¼ teaspoon freshly ground black
  pepper
Nonstick cooking spray

Combine all ingredients except cooking spray in a medium bowl. Mix well. Divide and shape crabmeat mixture into six patties. Cover with plastic wrap and chill for 1 hour.

Coat a large skillet with cooking spray and heat over medium heat. Add crabmeat patties and cook until golden brown, about 5 minutes per side.

Makes 6 servings

Nutritional Information per Serving (based on 6 servings)

Calories • 116	Calories from Fat • 13	Percent of Calories from Fat • 12%	Fat • 1.5g
Protein • 16.2g	Carbohydrate • 8.5g	Cholesterol • 63mg	Sodium • 504mg

LOUISIANA SHRIMP CREOLE

2 teaspoons margarine

2 stalks celery, chopped fine (1 cup)

1 medium onion, chopped fine (1 cup)

½ medium red bell pepper, chopped fine (½ cup)

1 medium green bell pepper, chopped fine

1 clove garlic, crushed

1 14-ounce can whole tomatoes, drained (juices reserved), cut up

2 tablespoons chopped fresh parsley

2 teaspoons Louisiana Seasoning Mix (see Index)

1 teaspoon allspice

2½ pounds medium raw shrimp, peeled and deveined

2 tablespoons cornstarch

3 tablespoons cold water

6 cups cooked long-grain white rice

Melt margarine in a large skillet. Sauté celery, onion, red and green pepper, and garlic until tender, about 10 minutes. Stir in tomatoes with their juice, parsley, Louisiana Seasoning Mix, and allspice. Bring to a boil, then add shrimp and return to a boil. Mix cornstarch with the cold water and add to the shrimp. Simmer for 8 minutes. Remove from heat and serve over cooked rice.

Makes 6 servings

LONG-GRAIN RICE

The length of "long-grain" rice is four times its width. Cooking long-grain rice results in light, dry grains that separate easily. Medium-grain rice has a higher starch content and is stickier. Most grocery stores carry mainly medium- and short-grain rice.

Nutritional Information per Serving (based on 6 servings)

Calories • 414	Calories from Fat • 33	Percent of Calories from Fat • 8%	Fat • 3.7g
Protein • 36.9g	Carbohydrate • 55.6g	Cholesterol • 292mg	Sodium • 467mg

SHRIMP ÉTOUFFÉE

⅔ cup Cajun Roux (see Index)

1 medium green bell pepper, chopped fine

1 medium onion, chopped fine

2 stalks celery, chopped fine (1 cup)

3 cloves garlic, minced

1¼ cups Chicken Broth (see Index)

¼ cup tomato paste

½ cup dry white wine

½ cup chopped scallion

½ teaspoon cayenne

2 bay leaves

1 teaspoon dried thyme

¼ cup chopped fresh parsley

2½ pounds medium raw shrimp, peeled and deveined

6 cups cooked long-grain white rice

In a large saucepan, combine roux, bell pepper, onion, celery, and garlic. Sauté for 10 minutes or until tender. Add chicken broth, tomato paste, and wine, and stir constantly until the mixture thickens. Stir in scallion, cayenne, bay leaves, and thyme. Cover and simmer for 40 minutes.

Stir in parsley and shrimp, then simmer, uncovered, for 20 additional minutes. Remove bay leaves and discard. Serve over rice.

Makes 6 servings

Nutritional Information per Serving (based on 6 servings)

Calories • 560	Calories from Fat • 106	Percent of Calories from Fat • 19%	Fat • 11.8g
Protein • 39.4g	Carbohydrate • 67.8g	Cholesterol • 294mg	Sodium • 437mg

SHRIMP SAUTÉ

½ cup white wine

1½ pounds medium raw shrimp, peeled and deveined

¼ cup chopped scallion

8 ounces snow peas

¾ teaspoon dried basil

1 teaspoon fresh chopped parsley

2 bay leaves

2 cloves garlic, whole

2 tablespoons cold water

1½ teaspoons cornstarch

1 teaspoon fresh lemon juice

1 tablespoon low-sodium soy sauce

⅛ teaspoon freshly ground black pepper

Salt

2 cups cooked long-grain white rice

Heat a large skillet over medium heat. Add wine and shrimp and cook for 5 minutes, stirring occasionally. Add scallion, snow peas, basil, parsley, bay leaves, and garlic. Cover and simmer for 5 minutes, stirring occasionally.

Combine water and cornstarch in a small bowl. Blend in lemon juice, soy sauce, and black pepper. Add cornstarch mixture to shrimp, and stir well. Bring to a boil, adjust seasoning, and cook, stirring constantly, until sauce is slightly thickened. Remove and discard bay leaves and garlic cloves. Serve over hot cooked rice.

Makes 4—6 servings

Nutritional Information per Serving (based on 6 servings)

Calories • 185	Calories from Fat • 11	Percent of Calories from Fat • 6%	Fat • 1.2g
Protein • 20.9g	Carbohydrate • 17.7g	Cholesterol • 175mg	Sodium • 288mg

Shrimp-Stuffed Peppers

1 teaspoon margarine
8 ounces ground turkey
1 cup finely chopped onion
1 stalk celery, chopped
2 cloves garlic, minced
2 tablespoons fresh chopped
  parsley
Salt
2 pounds medium shrimp, peeled,
  cleaned, and chopped fine

⅛ teaspoon freshly ground black
  pepper
1 cup cooked long–grain white
  rice
4½ cups cold water
8 medium green bell peppers
Nonstick cooking spray

In a large skillet, melt margarine over medium heat. Add ground turkey and cook until browned. Stir in onion, celery, garlic, and parsley. Cook 5 minutes or until tender, and salt to taste. Add shrimp, black pepper, and rice. Set aside.

Bring water to a boil in a large saucepan. Cut the top from each pepper; remove seeds and pulp. Lower peppers into boiling water and boil 5 minutes. Drain.

Preheat oven to 350°F. Coat a large baking dish with cooking spray. Fill each pepper with ¾ cup mixture, then arrange, filled side up, on baking dish. Bake for 35 minutes or until thoroughly heated.

Makes 8 servings

Nutritional Information per Serving (based on 8 servings)

Calories • 188	Calories from Fat • 41	Percent of Calories from Fat • 22%	Fat • 4.5g
Protein • 25g	Carbohydrate • 10.8g	Cholesterol • 189mg	Sodium • 231mg

QUICK AND SPICY SHRIMP

1 pound large shrimp, peeled and
   deveined, tail on
1 teaspoon canola oil
2 teaspoons garlic, minced
1 teaspoon Worcestershire sauce
2 tablespoons tomato paste
½ cup dry white wine

1 teaspoon dried basil
½ teaspoon dried oregano
½ teaspoon freshly ground black
   pepper
½ teaspoon cayenne
Salt

Rinse shrimp and set aside. Heat oil in a medium saucepan or deep skillet for 2 minutes. Add garlic and sauté for 45 seconds. Stir in Worcestershire sauce, tomato paste, and wine, and blend thoroughly. Add basil, oregano, black pepper, cayenne, and salt to taste. Bring to a boil, add shrimp, and cook over medium heat for 8 minutes, turning to thoroughly coat shrimp with sauce. Serve immediately, or cool and refrigerate to serve later.

Makes 4 servings

Nutritional Information per Serving (based on 4 servings)

Calories • 135	Calories from Fat • 20	Percent of Calories from Fat • 16%	Fat • 2.3g
Protein • 19.3g	Carbohydrate • 3.6g	Cholesterol • 175mg	Sodium • 277mg

Shrimp Curry

1½ pounds large shrimp, washed, peeled, and deveined
2 tablespoons fresh lemon juice
¼ teaspoon garlic powder
1 tablespoon vegetable oil
1 medium onion, chopped fine
½ medium red bell pepper, chopped fine

2 tablespoons curry powder
½ cup cold water
Salt
2 cups cooked long-grain white rice

Place shrimp in a medium plastic bowl. Combine lemon juice and garlic powder, and pour over shrimp. Let stand 10 minutes.

Heat oil in a large skillet, and sauté onion and bell pepper for 10 minutes, until tender. Stir in curry powder, then slowly add water, and simmer 15 minutes. Stir in shrimp and cook 15 minutes longer, until shrimp is done. Salt to taste, and serve over rice.

Makes 4 servings

Nutritional Information per Serving (based on 4 servings)

Calories • 303	Calories from Fat • 51	Percent of Calories from Fat • 17%	Fat • 5.7g
Protein • 31.4g	Carbohydrate • 30.4g	Cholesterol • 262mg	Sodium • 301mg

SMOTHERED CHICKEN

1 teaspoon vegetable oil
1½ teaspoons Cajun Spice Mix
  (see Index)
1 2- to 3-pound broiler-fryer, cut
  up, skin and all visible fat
  removed
Nonstick cooking spray
1 cup finely chopped onion

½ medium green bell pepper,
  chopped fine
2 16-ounce jars fat-free chicken
  gravy
2 cloves garlic, crushed
6 cups cooked long-grain white
  rice

Heat oil in a large nonstick skillet over medium heat. Sprinkle Cajun Spice Mix over chicken. Brown chicken on both sides until liquid from chicken runs clear, about 20 minutes. Remove from skillet.

Wash and dry skillet, and coat with cooking spray. Heat over medium heat, and cook onion and bell pepper, stirring constantly, until tender.

Return chicken to skillet. Add gravy and garlic, cover, and cook over low heat for 45 minutes, stirring occasionally. Serve over rice.

Makes 6 servings

Nutritional Information per Serving (based on 6 servings)

Calories • 903	Calories from Fat • 36	Percent of Calories from Fat • 5%	Fat • 3.9g
Protein • 15g	Carbohydrate • 148.3g	Cholesterol • 33mg	Sodium • 945mg

OVEN-FRIED CHICKEN

4 chicken drumsticks, skin and
  all visible fat removed
4 chicken thighs, skin and all
  visible fat removed
2 whole chicken breasts, skin and
  all visible fat removed
Nonstick cooking spray
1 cup dried herb-flavored bread
  crumbs

1 cup all-purpose flour
¼ cup fine yellow cornmeal
3½ tablespoons Cajun Spice Mix
  (see Index)
Dash cayenne
1 cup nonfat plain yogurt

Wash and dry chicken pieces, then chill in a large bowl until needed. Preheat oven to 400°F. Coat a large baking sheet with cooking spray. Combine bread crumbs, flour, cornmeal, Cajun Spice Mix, and cayenne in a large zip-top plastic bag. Seal well and shake to blend.

Remove three pieces of chilled chicken from bowl. (Leave others in refrigerator until needed.) Coat one chicken piece at a time with yogurt, then place in bag of coating mix and seal. Shake to coat thoroughly. Place coated chicken on baking sheet, then repeat the process for remaining pieces.

Spray chicken with cooking spray, and bake on bottom rack of oven for 1 hour, turning pieces every 20 minutes.

Makes 10 servings

Nutritional Information per Serving (based on 10 servings)

Calories • 230	Calories from Fat • 47	Percent of Calories from Fat • 21%	Fat • 5.2g
Protein • 24.8g	Carbohydrate • 19.4g	Cholesterol • 66mg	Sodium • 484mg

CHICKEN AND DUMPLINGS

1 5-pound stewing chicken, cut up, skin and all visible fat removed

1½ quarts Chicken Broth (see Index)

1 medium onion, chopped (1 cup)

1 medium green bell pepper, chopped (1 cup)

2 cloves garlic, crushed

1 teaspoon celery seed

1 teaspoon freshly ground black pepper

Dumplings

2½ cups all-purpose flour

1 teaspoon dried parsley flakes

2 teaspoons sugar

2 teaspoons baking powder

¼ cup cholesterol-free egg substitute

1½ cups skim milk

½ teaspoon salt

¼ cup low-fat plain yogurt

Wash chicken pieces; drain well. Place chicken in a large pot or dutch oven with chicken broth, onion, bell pepper, garlic, celery seed, and black pepper. Bring to a boil, reduce heat, cover, and simmer 2½ hours. (Liquid should just cover the chicken and vegetables; add more water if needed.)

In a medium bowl, mix together remaining ingredients. Blend to form a smooth, soft dough.

With lightly floured hands, roll dough into 1-inch balls (or spoon up with a tablespoon). Drop dumplings into simmering chicken mixture until they cover the surface in a single layer. Cover and let boil for 15 minutes. Reduce heat and simmer 5 minutes more, until the dumplings are light and cooked through.

Makes 6 servings

Nutritional Information per Serving (based on 6 servings)

Calories • 444	Calories from Fat • 76	Percent of Calories from Fat • 18%	Fat • 8.4g
Protein • 39.4g	Carbohydrate • 50g	Cholesterol • 93mg	Sodium • 447mg

French Quarter Chicken Breasts

6 4- to 6-ounce skinless, boneless chicken breast halves (visible fat removed)
2 cups fat-free Italian salad dressing
3 tablespoons Salt-Free Cajun Seasoning Blend (see Index)
Nonstick cooking spray
1 tablespoon canola oil

½ medium green bell pepper, julienned
½ medium yellow bell pepper, julienned
½ medium red bell pepper, julienned
1 medium yellow onion, julienned

GARLIC

What's a southern dish without this spice? Buy tightly closed bulbs with unwrinkled skins, and store them in a cool, dark place. To peel garlic, place a clove under the broad side of a chef's knife, then thump on the blade to split the skin. The skin will then slip away easily. Remove pulp and chop to desired size, or mash through a press.

Wash chicken breasts and pat dry. Arrange in a baking dish. Mix Italian dressing and Salt-Free Cajun Seasoning Blend. Pour over chicken. Cover and refrigerate for 4 hours.

Remove chicken from marinade. Spray a cast-iron skillet with nonfat cooking spray. Add the chicken and cook until just browned.

Meanwhile, heat the canola oil in a large nonstick skillet. Add the green, yellow, and red pepper with onion and sauté while chicken is cooking. Serve chicken topped with pepper and onion.

Makes 6 servings

Nutritional Information per Serving (based on 6 servings)

Calories • 209	Calories from Fat • 48	Percent of Calories from Fat • 25%	Fat • 5.3g
Protein • 26g	Carbohydrate • 10.5g	Cholesterol • 69mg	Sodium • 1,456mg

CAJUN CHICKEN AND "DIRTY" RICE

1 tablespoon canola oil
8 ounces chicken gizzards, chopped fine
8 ounces chicken liver, chopped fine
2 4- to 6-ounce cooked skinless, boneless chicken breasts, cut into ½-inch cubes
1½ medium onions, diced fine
½ cup finely diced celery

½ medium green bell pepper, diced
2 cloves garlic, minced
2 tablespoons salt
1 teaspoon freshly ground black pepper
⅛ teaspoon cayenne
3 cups cooked long-grain white rice
½ cup chopped fresh parsley

Heat oil in a large skillet over medium heat. Brown gizzards and liver. Add chicken breast, onion, celery, bell pepper, garlic, salt, black pepper, and cayenne. Mix well, then cover and cook, stirring occasionally, about 10 minutes or until vegetables are tender. Stir in rice and parsley. Continue cooking, mixing lightly, for 5 minutes.

Makes 8 servings

Nutritional Information per Serving (based on 8 servings)

Calories • 233	Calories from Fat • 46	Percent of Calories from Fat • 20%	Fat • 5.1g
Protein • 24.4g	Carbohydrate • 20.9g	Cholesterol • 181mg	Sodium • 595mg

COUNTRY CHICKEN

1 3- to 3½-pound broiler-fryer,
skin and all visible fat removed

1 tablespoon margarine

1 10½-ounce can condensed
chicken broth, defatted

¼ teaspoon dried thyme

¼ teaspoon freshly ground black
pepper

8 medium carrots, quartered
lengthwise

8 pearl onions

4 medium turnips, quartered
lengthwise

½ cup Chicken Broth (see Index)

2 tablespoons cold water

1 tablespoon cornstarch

Fold chicken wings across back. Tie drumsticks together. Melt margarine in a nonstick dutch oven and cook chicken until brown on all sides. Drain.

Preheat oven to 375°F. Pour condensed broth over chicken, and sprinkle with thyme and pepper. Cover and bake 45 minutes.

Arrange carrot quarters, onions, and turnip quarters around chicken. Cover and bake 1½ hours longer or until juices of chicken run clear.

Remove chicken and vegetables, and skim fat from drippings in dutch oven. Stir ½ cup chicken broth into remaining juices and heat to boiling. Blend together water and cornstarch and stir into broth mixture. Bring to a boil and stir constantly for 1 to 2 minutes. Arrange chicken and vegetables on a large platter and serve with sauce on the side.

Makes 6 servings

Nutritional Information per Serving (based on 6 servings)

Calories • 197	Calories from Fat • 57	Percent of Calories from Fat • 28%	Fat • 6.3g
Protein • 19.1g	Carbohydrate • 17.2g	Cholesterol • 50mg	Sodium • 231mg

CHICKEN AND KIDNEY BEANS

1 cup dried kidney beans

2 tablespoons vegetable oil

1 3- to 3½-pound broiler-fryer, cut into 6 pieces, skin and all visible fat removed

¼ cup finely chopped green bell pepper

1 stalk celery, sliced thin

1 medium onion, chopped fine

¼ teaspoon seasoning salt

½ teaspoon dried thyme

1 16-ounce can chopped tomatoes

1 cup Chicken Broth (see Index)

1 large clove garlic, chopped fine

In a small bowl, cover beans with water and soak 2 hours; drain. Heat oil in a nonstick dutch oven or heavy 12-inch skillet. Cook chicken over medium heat about 15 minutes, until light brown on all sides, then drain off fat. Stir in remaining ingredients. Bring to a boil, reduce heat, and cover. Simmer for 40 to 50 minutes or until juices of chicken run clear and beans are tender.

Makes 6 servings

Nutritional Information per Serving (based on 6 servings)

Calories • 281	Calories from Fat • 84	Percent of Calories from Fat • 29%	Fat • 9.3g
Protein • 24.9g	Carbohydrate • 25.2g	Cholesterol • 51mg	Sodium • 245mg

Pepper Chicken

1 3-pound broiler-fryer, cut into 8 pieces, skin and all visible fat removed
¼ cup light soy sauce
3 tablespoons cold water
1 clove garlic, chopped fine
1 8-ounce can sliced water chestnuts, drained

½ medium red bell pepper, cut into 1-inch pieces
1 medium green bell pepper, cut into 1-inch pieces
2 tablespoons cornstarch

Place chicken in a nonstick dutch oven or heavy 12-inch skillet. Mix soy sauce with 1 tablespoon of the water and pour over chicken. Bring to a boil, reduce heat, and simmer, uncovered, 40 to 50 minutes. Add garlic, water chestnuts, and red and green pepper. Cover again and simmer 10 minutes longer, until juices from chicken run clear. Remove chicken to serving dish, and keep warm.

Blend together cornstarch and remaining 2 tablespoons of water. Stir into juices in dutch oven and heat, stirring constantly, until mixture thickens and boils. Boil and stir 2 minutes.

Serve chicken and sauce over cooked rice or pasta.

Makes 6 servings

Nutritional Information per Serving (based on 6 servings)

Calories • 142	Calories from Fat • 38	Percent of Calories from Fat • 27%	Fat • 4.2g
Protein • 17.6g	Carbohydrate • 8.2g	Cholesterol • 49mg	Sodium • 403mg

CHICKEN CURRY

1 3-pound boiler-fryer, cut up, skin and all visible fat removed

1 tablespoon plus 2 teaspoons margarine

1½ cups Chicken Broth (see Index)

1 medium onion, chopped fine

1 clove garlic, chopped fine

2 tablespoons curry powder

1 medium apple, peeled and chopped fine

¼ cup all-purpose flour

¼ teaspoon ground cardamom

½ teaspoon ground ginger

1 teaspoon salt

½ teaspoon freshly ground black pepper

2 teaspoons grated lime peel

2 tablespoons lime juice

6 cups cooked long-grain white rice

Wash chicken and pat dry. Melt 2 teaspoons of the margarine in a large skillet, and brown chicken pieces on all sides. Add chicken broth and bring to a boil. Reduce heat and simmer for 30 minutes. Remove chicken and keep warm. Add enough water to the skillet to make about 3 cups of liquid.

In another large skillet, melt remaining tablespoon of margarine and sauté onion, garlic, curry powder, and apple until onion is tender. Stir in flour, cardamom, ginger, salt, and pepper. Gradually stir in reserved liquid plus lime peel and lime juice. Bring to a boil, reduce heat, and simmer 25 minutes. Stir in chicken and heat lightly. Serve over rice.

Makes 6 servings

Nutritional Information per Serving (based on 6 servings)

Calories • 190	Calories from Fat • 71	Percent of Calories from Fat • 37%	Fat • 7.9g
Protein • 18.1g	Carbohydrate • 11.9g	Cholesterol • 52mg	Sodium • 447mg

Turkey-Stuffed Bell peppers

6 large green bell peppers
½ teaspoon salt
Nonstick cooking spray
2 pounds ground turkey
1 medium onion, chopped fine
   (1 cup)
1 8-ounce can tomato sauce
1 cup cooked long-grain white
   rice

½ teaspoon dried thyme
¼ teaspoon freshly ground black
   pepper
¼ teaspoon garlic powder
2 tablespoons Worcestershire
   sauce

Cut the stem end from the bell peppers, and remove the seeds and white fiber. Wash peppers well, and place in an 8-quart pot of boiling water. Add salt, and return the water to a boil. Boil, uncovered, for 10 minutes. Drain water from peppers.

Coat a large baking dish with cooking spray. Place peppers in dish, open side up. Coat a large skillet with cooking spray, and heat over medium heat. Sauté ground turkey and onion until light brown, breaking up turkey as it cooks. Stir in tomato sauce, rice, thyme, black pepper, garlic powder, and Worcestershire sauce. Cook 5 to 8 minutes, until well blended.

Preheat oven to 375°F. Spoon mixture evenly into bell pepper shells. Bake, uncovered, for 30 minutes, until lightly browned on top.

Makes 6 servings

Nutritional Information per Serving (based on 6 servings)

Calories • 332	Calories from Fat • 140	Percent of Calories from Fat • 42%	Fat • 15.5g
Protein • 29.1g	Carbohydrate • 18.3g	Cholesterol • 76mg	Sodium • 549mg

TURKEY WINGS AND GRAVY

6—8 turkey wings (about 3½ pounds)

2 stalks celery, cut into ½-inch slices

1 small onion, sliced thin

2 cloves garlic, crushed

1 medium green bell pepper, cut into ¼-inch rings

1½ teaspoons poultry seasoning

2 teaspoons Cajun Spice Mix (see Index)

2 16-ounce jars fat-free brown gravy

Salt and black pepper

6 cups cooked long-grain white rice

Cut each turkey wing into three pieces (at the joints), and discard the tips. Remove as much skin as possible. Place wing pieces, celery, onion, garlic, and bell pepper in a large pot with enough cold water to cover the wings. Add poultry seasoning and Cajun Spice Mix. Bring to a boil, reduce heat, and simmer until wings are tender, about 20 minutes. Stir in brown gravy, and cook for 1 hour over low heat, adding water if necessary to prevent scorching. If gravy becomes too thick, add more water to thin. Adjust seasoning and serve over rice.

Makes 6 servings

Nutritional Information per Serving (based on 6 servings)

Calories • 711	Calories from Fat • 213	Percent of Calories from Fat • 31%	Fat • 23.7g
Protein • 58.3g	Carbohydrate • 58.2g	Cholesterol • 150mg	Sodium • 1,227mg

Turkey and Peppers

2 turkey thighs (2½ pounds), skin and bones removed

Nonstick cooking spray

½ cup plus 1 tablespoon cold water

2 tablespoons fresh chopped parsley

2 tablespoons low–sodium soy sauce

½ teaspoon dried thyme

¼ teaspoon dried rosemary

1 medium green bell pepper, cut into ¼-inch strips

1 medium red bell pepper, cut into ¼-inch strips

¼ cup chopped scallion

1 teaspoon cornstarch

Cut turkey into strips. Coat a large nonstick skillet with cooking spray. Add turkey and cook over medium heat about 8 minutes, stirring occasionally. Stir in ½ cup of the water, parsley, soy sauce, thyme, and rosemary. Bring to a boil, reduce heat, cover, and simmer about 35 minutes or until turkey is tender. Stir in green and red pepper and scallion. Cover and simmer 5 minutes. Blend together cornstarch and remaining tablespoon of water. Stir into turkey mixture, and heat to boiling. Cook, stirring constantly, for 2 minutes.

Makes 6 servings

Nutritional Information per Serving (based on 6 servings)

Calories • 281	Calories from Fat • 91	Percent of Calories from Fat • 33%	Fat • 10.1g
Protein • 40.7g	Carbohydrate • 4.9g	Cholesterol • 117mg	Sodium • 286mg

TURKEY BREAKFAST SAUSAGE

1½ pounds ground turkey
¼ cup finely chopped shallots
3 tablespoons finely chopped
   fresh parsley
2 tablespoons fresh lemon juice

1 teaspoon Cajun Spice Mix (see
   Index)
¼ teaspoon ground cloves
¾ cup unsweetened applesauce
Nonstick cooking spray

Combine all ingredients except cooking spray in a large bowl and mix well. Shape into 12 patties. Cover and refrigerate 2 to 4 hours.

Coat a large nonstick skillet with cooking spray, and heat over medium heat. Cook patties until golden brown, 5 to 6 minutes on each side, adding a small amount of water if necessary to prevent sticking. Test for doneness by removing a patty from the pan and piercing the center with a knife. Sausage is done when center is no longer pink and juices run clear.

Makes 6 servings

Nutritional Information per Serving (based on 6 servings)

Calories • 209	Calories from Fat • 103	Percent of Calories from Fat • 50%	Fat • 11.4g
Protein • 20.4g	Carbohydrate • 5.2g	Cholesterol • 57mg	Sodium • 102mg

5

VEGETABLES

Baked Green Beans

Crowder Peas

Vegetable and Rice—Stuffed Bell Peppers

Cajun Pepper Sauté

Southern Fried Okra

Smothered Okra

Creole Stewed Okra and Tomatoes

Succotash

Fried Green Tomatoes

Sautéed Pearl Onions

Vegetable Jambalaya

Mustard Greens with Turkey Ham

Collard Greens

Turnip Greens

Down-Home Cabbage

Stuffed Eggplant

Smothered Corn

Potato-Onion Casserole

Cajun Zucchini

Sautéed Mushrooms and Garlic

In traditional southern cooking, vegetables are usually overcooked in large quantities of water. The nutritional value of the vegetables is greatly diminished, but the cooking juices retain the nutrients. In the South, this juice is called "pot likker," and it's served right in the dish with the vegetables.

Cooked for hours on end, traditional southern vegetable dishes have always tasted wonderful. Herbs are used extensively in the Cajun and Creole vegetable dishes, and their distinctive flavors will convert even the most skeptical taste buds. From baked beans to zucchini, vegetables are a mainstay of the Cajun–Creole diet.

Baked Green Beans

1½ pounds fresh green beans
Nonstick cooking spray
1 tablespoon light olive oil

1 clove garlic, chopped fine
¼ teaspoon Cajun Spice Mix (see
   Index)

Preheat oven to 400°F. Place the green beans on a baking dish coated lightly with cooking spray. Drizzle beans with oil, add garlic, and toss lightly. Sprinkle with Cajun Spice Mix, and bake until beans are shriveled and browned, about 30 to 40 minutes. Serve hot.

Makes 4 servings

Nutritional Information per Serving (based on 4 servings)

Calories • 90	Calories from Fat • 35	Percent of Calories from Fat • 34%	Fat • 3.9g
Protein • 3.3g	Carbohydrate • 13.7g	Cholesterol • 0mg	Sodium • 16.7mg

CROWDER PEAS

6 cups shelled crowder peas

2 medium onions, chopped fine

1 medium green bell pepper, chopped fine

3 tablespoons finely minced parsley

2 cloves garlic, minced fine

1 pound turkey ham, cut into 1-inch cubes

1 teaspoon Cajun Spice Mix (see Index)

2 bay leaves

7 cups cold water

8 cups cooked long-grain white rice

Rinse peas under cold water. Combine peas, onion, bell pepper, parsley, garlic, turkey ham, Cajun Spice Mix, and bay leaves in a heavy stock-pot. Add cold water to cover. Bring to a boil, reduce heat, and simmer 2 to 2½ hours, until peas are tender and a natural gravy has formed. Stir frequently during cooking, scraping the sides and bottom of the pot to prevent scorching. If the mixture appears too dry, add about ⅔ cup to 1 cup of water 15 minutes before the end of cooking. Remove and discard bay leaves. Serve over rice.

Makes 8—10 servings

Nutritional Information per Serving (based on 10 servings)

Calories • 364	Calories from Fat • 46	Percent of Calories from Fat • 13%	Fat • 5.1g
Protein • 18.5g	Carbohydrate • 59.2g	Cholesterol • 25mg	Sodium • 668mg

Vegetable and Rice–Stuffed Bell Peppers

3 medium green bell peppers, cut
  in half lengthwise
1½ cups cooked long-grain white
  rice
4 scallions with tops, chopped
  fine
1 medium tomato, chopped fine
⅓ cup finely chopped celery
1 teaspoon chili powder

¾ teaspoon salt
Nonstick cooking spray
¼ cup ketchup
6 1-ounce slices fat-free cheddar
  cheese
6 1-ounce slices fat-free Swiss
  cheese
¼ cup cold water

Preheat oven to 350°F. In a large saucepan, boil enough water to cover
peppers. Lower peppers into boiling water, and boil 5 minutes. Drain and
rinse in cold water.

In a large mixing bowl, stir together rice, scallion, tomato, celery, chili
powder, and salt. Fill pepper halves with rice mixture.

Coat a 9-inch square baking pan with cooking spray. Arrange peppers in pan, and drizzle ketchup over tops. Top each pepper with 1 slice
of each of the cheeses. Pour water into bottom of pan, and bake, uncovered, for 25 to 30 minutes, until heated through.

Makes 6 servings

Nutritional Information per Serving (based on 6 servings)

Calories • 166	Calories from Fat • 4	Percent of Calories from Fat • 2%	Fat • 0.4g
Protein • 17.7g	Carbohydrate • 22.9g	Cholesterol • 0mg	Sodium • 992mg

CAJUN PEPPER SAUTÉ

Nonstick cooking spray

1 tablespoon cold water

2 teaspoons vegetable oil

1 medium green bell pepper, cut lengthwise into strips

1 medium red bell pepper, cut lengthwise into strips

1 medium yellow bell pepper, cut lengthwise into strips

2 cloves garlic, crushed

¼ teaspoon Cajun Spice Mix (see Index)

2 tablespoons fresh lemon juice

Coat a large skillet with cooking spray. Add water and oil, and heat over medium–high heat until hot. Add green, red, and yellow pepper, garlic, and Cajun Spice Mix. Sauté 3 to 5 minutes, stirring constantly. Remove from heat, and stir in lemon juice.

Try this over cooked rice or as a side dish with poultry.

Makes 6 servings

Nutritional Information per Serving (based on 6 servings)

Calories • 41	Calories from Fat • 16	Percent of Calories from Fat • 34%	Fat • 1.7g
Protein • 1.1g	Carbohydrate • 6.5g	Cholesterol • 0mg	Sodium • 9mg

Southern Fried Okra

1 pound fresh whole baby okra
Salt to taste
Freshly ground black pepper

1 tablespoon vegetable oil
Nonstick cooking spray
Tabasco

Wash okra, remove stems, and cut into ½-inch slices. In a large bowl, combine okra, salt, pepper, and oil. Lightly coat a large skillet with cooking spray. Cook okra mixture over medium heat, turning with spatula to cook evenly. Cook until okra is tender and browned, about 10 minutes. Serve with Tabasco.

Makes 6 servings

Nutritional Information per Serving (based on 6 servings)

Calories • 45	Calories from Fat • 22	Percent of Calories from Fat • 44%	Fat • 2.4g
Protein • 1.4g	Carbohydrate • 5.5g	Cholesterol • 0mg	Sodium • 4mg

SMOTHERED OKRA

1 teaspoon canola oil
2 medium onions, sliced thin
2 cloves garlic, minced
1 medium green bell pepper, chopped fine

2 pounds fresh okra, trimmed and cut into ½-inch slices
2 teaspoons Cajun Spice Mix (see Index)
2 medium tomatoes, chopped fine

Heat oil in a heavy skillet over medium heat. Add onion, garlic, and bell pepper, and cook about 10 minutes or until tender, stirring frequently. Add okra, Cajun Spice Mix, and tomato, and sauté for 15 minutes more. Reduce heat and cover. Simmer for 30 to 40 minutes, stirring frequently, until okra is tender.

Makes 4 servings

Nutritional Information per Serving (based on 4 servings)

Calories • 134	Calories from Fat • 17	Percent of Calories from Fat • 11%	Fat • 1.9g
Protein • 6g	Carbohydrate • 27.9g	Cholesterol • 0mg	Sodium • 112mg

Creole Stewed Okra and Tomatoes

2 teaspoons vegetable oil
1 medium onion, cut in half
  lengthwise and sliced thin
3 cloves garlic, minced fine
1 28-ounce can peeled, diced
  tomatoes

2 10-ounce packages frozen
  whole okra
½ teaspoon Cajun Spice Mix (see
  Index)

Heat oil in a heavy 3-quart saucepan over medium heat. Combine remaining ingredients, and stir until well blended. Simmer, stirring often, about 45 minutes, until mixture is very soft. Adjust seasoning to taste.

Makes 4—6 servings

Nutritional Information per Serving (based on 6 servings)

Calories • 83	Calories from Fat • 18	Percent of Calories from Fat • 20%	Fat • 2.0g
Protein • 3.4g	Carbohydrate • 15.3g	Cholesterol • 0mg	Sodium • 237mg

SUCCOTASH

4 smoked turkey wings (about 2
  pounds), cut in half
6 cups cold water
1 pound fresh green beans
1 medium onion, chopped fine
Salt and freshly ground black
  pepper to taste

6 small new potatoes (1 pound),
  washed and quartered
1 pound fresh okra, trimmed and
  cut into ½-inch slices
1 10-ounce package frozen lima
  beans
1 cup fresh or frozen corn

Place turkey wings and water in a large stockpot. Bring to a boil, reduce heat, and simmer for 1½ hours. Wash green beans, and break into three pieces each. Add green beans, onion, salt, and pepper to stockpot, and simmer, covered, for 20 minutes. Add potatoes, okra, lima beans, and corn. If succotash is too thick, add 1 to 1½ cups of water. Simmer until potatoes are tender, about 15 minutes. Adjust seasoning if necessary.

Makes 6—8 servings

Nutritional Information per Serving (based on 8 servings)

Calories • 339	Calories from Fat • 122	Percent of Calories from Fat • 35%	Fat • 13.6g
Protein • 20.2g	Carbohydrate • 37g	Cholesterol • 0mg	Sodium • 926mg

Fried Green Tomatoes

3 large green tomatoes, cut into
   ½-inch slices
Salt-Free Cajun Seasoning Blend
   (see Index)
¼ cup fine yellow cornmeal

¼ cup all-purpose flour
3 egg whites (or ½ cup
   cholesterol-free egg substitute)
Nonstick cooking spray
2 teaspoons vegetable oil

Sprinkle both sides of tomato slices with Salt-Free Cajun Seasoning
Blend. Mix the cornmeal and flour together in a small bowl. Dredge
tomato slices in egg white, then in the cornmeal-flour mixture until completely coated. Arrange slices on a plate or wire rack, and let stand 5 to
10 minutes.

   Coat a large skillet with cooking spray, add 1 teaspoon of the oil, and
heat over medium heat. Slowly slip tomato slices into skillet. (Do not
crowd.) Cook, turning once, until tomatoes are golden brown on both
sides, about 5 minutes. Repeat with remaining tomato slices, recoating
skillet with vegetable cooking spray and remaining oil.

Makes 6 servings

Nutritional Information per Serving (based on 6 servings)

Calories • 74	Calories from Fat • 17	Percent of Calories from Fat • 22%	Fat • 1.9g
Protein • 3.5g	Carbohydrate • 11.2g	Cholesterol • 0mg	Sodium • 37mg

SAUTÉED PEARL ONIONS

2 teaspoons margarine
1½ pounds pearl onions, skins
   and hard ends removed
1 teaspoon ground coriander
¾ teaspoon salt
½ teaspoon freshly ground white
   pepper

1 5⅓-ounce can (⅔ cup)
   evaporated skim milk
¼ cup brown sugar
1 cinnamon stick
½ teaspoon dried basil

In a large, heavy skillet, melt margarine over low heat. Sauté onions, coriander, salt, and pepper, stirring frequently, until onions begin to brown. Increase heat slightly and continue to cook, stirring constantly to avoid burning. Stir in milk, brown sugar, cinnamon, and basil. Increase heat again and continue to cook, stirring constantly, for 5 minutes. Reduce heat, and simmer until liquid is reduced by half and onions are slightly glazed. Onions are done when they are easily pierced with a fork. Remove cinnamon stick before serving.

Makes 4 servings

Nutritional Information per Serving (based on 4 servings)

Calories • 210	Calories from Fat • 18	Percent of Calories from Fat • 8%	Fat • 2g
Protein • 5.4g	Carbohydrate • 43g	Cholesterol • 1mg	Sodium • 497mg

Vegetable Jambalaya

2 teaspoons canola oil
1 medium onion, diced fine
3 cloves garlic, minced
¾ cup finely diced celery
½ cup finely diced carrots
1 teaspoon dried thyme
½ teaspoon salt
Pinch cayenne
1 bay leaf
1 medium red bell pepper, cut
  into ½-inch squares

1 medium green bell pepper, cut
  into ½-inch squares
1 cup cooked black-eyed peas
1 28-ounce can chopped tomatoes
3¼ cups chicken or vegetable
  broth, defatted
1½ cups uncooked long-grain
  white rice

Heat oil in a large, heavy dutch oven over low heat. Add onion and cook for 15 minutes, stirring frequently. Add garlic, celery, and carrot and cook, stirring frequently, 5 minutes longer. Add remaining ingredients except rice. Bring to a boil, reduce heat to medium-low, and cook, partially covered, for 10 minutes. Adjust seasoning if necessary, then stir in rice. Cover, reduce heat to low, and cook for 20 more minutes. (Do not cook dish longer than 20 minutes after adding rice.) Remove bay leaf before serving.

Makes 6 servings

Nutritional Information per Serving (based on 6 servings)

Calories • 288	Calories from Fat • 24	Percent of Calories from Fat • 8%	Fat • 2.6g
Protein • 10.6g	Carbohydrate • 56.8g	Cholesterol • 0mg	Sodium • 597mg

MUSTARD GREENS WITH TURKEY HAM

2 pounds mustard greens
1 teaspoon freshly ground black
   pepper
½ teaspoon dried red pepper
   flakes

2 quarts cold water
12 ounces turkey ham, cut into
   ½-inch cubes (1 cup)
Salt

Wash greens thoroughly, discarding stems and yellow leaves. Cut into small pieces. Put greens, black pepper, and red pepper flakes into an 8-quart pot. Add water, cover, and simmer 30 minutes. Add turkey ham and simmer 30 minutes longer, or until greens are tender. Add salt to taste.

Makes 4 servings

Nutritional Information per Serving (based on 4 servings)

| Calories • 145 | Calories from Fat • 44 | Percent of Calories from Fat • 29% | Fat • 4.9g |
| Protein • 21.3g | Carbohydrate • 5.6g | Cholesterol • 48mg | Sodium • 897mg |

Collard Greens

2 pounds collard greens
1 large onion, chopped fine
1 teaspoon freshly ground black
  pepper
½ teaspoon cayenne

2 quarts cold water
6 ounces turkey ham, cut into
  ½-inch cubes (about 1 cup)
Salt

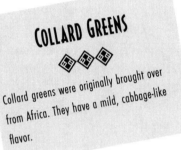

Collard Greens

Collard greens were originally brought over from Africa. They have a mild, cabbage-like flavor.

Wash greens thoroughly, discarding stems and yellow leaves. Cut into small pieces. Put greens, onion, black pepper, and cayenne into an 8-quart pot. Add water, cover, and simmer 30 minutes. Add turkey ham and simmer 30 minutes longer, or until greens are tender. Add salt to taste.

Makes 4 servings

Nutritional Information per Serving (based on 4 servings)

Calories • 123	Calories from Fat • 24	Percent of Calories from Fat • 18%	Fat • 2.6g
Protein • 11.2g	Carbohydrate • 15.9g	Cholesterol • 24mg	Sodium • 470mg

TURNIP GREENS

3 pounds turnip greens
3 cups cold water
2 cups Chicken Broth (see Index)
1 pound white turnips, peeled
    and cut into ½-inch cubes

1 pound smoked turkey ham, cut
    into ½-inch cubes
Sugar
Salt

Wash greens thoroughly, discarding stems and yellow leaves. Cut into small pieces. In a large pot, bring water and broth to a boil. Add greens, cover, and simmer for 1 hour. Add turnips and turkey ham. Cover and cook for an additional 30 minutes, until turnips are soft. Add sugar and salt to taste.

Makes 4—6 servings

Nutritional Information per Serving (based on 6 servings)

Calories • 246	Calories from Fat • 115	Percent of Calories from Fat • 45%	Fat • 12.8g
Protein • 17.2g	Carbohydrate • 18.7g	Cholesterol • 3mg	Sodium • 929mg

Down-Home Cabbage

1 large head cabbage, core
  removed
1 quart cold water
1 medium onion, chopped fine
12 ounces turkey ham, cut into
  ½-inch cubes (1 cup)

2 large potatoes, washed, peeled,
  and diced fine
1 teaspoon salt
1 teaspoon freshly ground black
  pepper

Remove any wilted or discolored outer leaves from cabbage, then shred.
In a large stockpot or dutch oven, bring water to a boil. Add all ingredients, reduce heat to low, cover, and cook until potato and cabbage are
tender, about 30 minutes. Stir occasionally during cooking, and add more
water if necessary.

Makes 4 servings

Nutritional Information per Serving (based on 4 servings)

Calories • 239	Calories from Fat • 38	Percent of Calories from Fat • 15%	Fat • 4.3g
Protein • 22.6g	Carbohydrate • 31.5g	Cholesterol • 75mg	Sodium • 1,559mg

STUFFED EGGPLANT

1 medium eggplant
⅔ cup cold water
1 beef bouillon cube
⅔ cup instant rice
8 ounces ground turkey
1 teaspoon Cajun Spice Mix (see
   Index)

1 10¾-ounce can condensed
   tomato soup
2 1-ounce slices fat-free cheddar
   cheese

Wash eggplant, cut in half lengthwise, and scoop pulp into a saucepan. Place eggplant halves in baking dish. Cook pulp in a small amount of boiling water about 5 minutes or until tender. Drain and mash.

In another saucepan, bring ⅔ cup water and bouillon cube to a boil. Add rice, stir, and remove from heat. Cover and let stand 5 minutes.

Preheat oven to 350°F. Heat a large skillet over medium heat and brown ground turkey, stirring occasionally. Remove skillet from heat. Stir in Cajun Spice Mix, rice, and mashed eggplant. Stuff eggplant shells with equal amounts of rice mixture. Spoon tomato soup on top, and bake 15 minutes. Top with cheese and bake 10 minutes longer, until cheese is melted.

Makes 2 servings

Nutritional Information per Serving (based on 2 servings)

Calories • 537	Calories from Fat • 135	Percent of Calories from Fat • 25%	Fat • 15g
Protein • 35g	Carbohydrate • 66g	Cholesterol • 59mg	Sodium • 1,750mg

SMOTHERED CORN

8 medium ears fresh corn

Nonstick cooking spray

½ medium green bell pepper, chopped

1 medium yellow onion, chopped

1 medium tomato, diced

¼ teaspoon cayenne

½ teaspoon freshly ground black pepper

½ teaspoon salt

Using a sharp knife, cut corn (about 4 cups) from cob. Coat a large skillet with cooking spray, and cook bell pepper and onion for 5 minutes, until tender. Stir in remaining ingredients. Cover skillet and reduce heat to low. Cook 25 minutes or until corn is tender.

Makes 6 servings

Nutritional Information per Serving (based on 6 servings)

Calories • 128	Calories from Fat • 13	Percent of Calories from Fat • 9%	Fat • 1.5g
Protein • 4g	Carbohydrate • 29.5g	Cholesterol • 0mg	Sodium • 198mg

POTATO-ONION CASSEROLE

Nonstick cooking spray

1 large white onion, cut into ⅛-inch-thick slices

2 cloves garlic, chopped fine

3½ tablespoons finely chopped fresh thyme

1 teaspoon salt, or to taste

Freshly ground black pepper

4 large baking potatoes, peeled and cut into ⅛-inch-thick slices

½ cup low-fat Parmesan cheese

½ cup fat-free sour cream

1 cup chicken broth or stock, defatted

Preheat oven to 375°F. Coat a large baking dish generously with cooking spray. Mix together onion, garlic, thyme, salt, and pepper. Layer the ingredients in the baking dish in the following order:

¼ of the potato slices

⅓ of the onion mixture

¼ of the Parmesan cheese

Repeat layers, ending with potato slices, then add sour cream and sprinkle with remaining Parmesan cheese. Pour broth into pan at sides until it comes about halfway up. Bake 1 hour, until potato and onion are tender.

Makes 6—8 servings

Nutritional Information per Serving (based on 8 servings)

Calories • 113	Calories from Fat • 8	Percent of Calories from Fat • 7%	Fat • 0.9g
Protein • 5.6g	Carbohydrate • 22.1g	Cholesterol • 0mg	Sodium • 415mg

Cajun Zucchini

1 cup Chicken Broth (see Index)

2 teaspoons cornstarch

2 medium zucchini, cut into
   ¼-inch slices (3 cups)

2 teaspoons paprika

½ teaspoon dried thyme

½ teaspoon dried oregano

⅛ teaspoon cayenne

Mix ¼ cup of the chicken broth with the cornstarch in a small bowl. Set aside. In a 10-inch skillet over medium heat, cook remaining broth and other ingredients, stirring occasionally, until zucchini is tender, about 10 minutes. Stir in cornstarch mixture and cook, stirring, about 3 minutes, until thickened.

Makes 6 servings

Nutritional Information per Serving (based on 6 servings)

| Calories • 19 | Calories from Fat • 2 | Percent of Calories from Fat • 8% | Fat • 0.2g |
| Protein • 1.7g | Carbohydrate • 3.5g | Cholesterol • 0mg | Sodium • 58mg |

SAUTÉED MUSHROOMS AND GARLIC

1 teaspoon butter
¼ cup white wine vinegar
6 cups fresh whole mushrooms
2 cloves garlic, crushed
1 small red onion, sliced thin

2 tablespoons finely chopped
 parsley
Salt
⅛ teaspoon cracked black pepper

Melt butter over low heat in a heavy skillet. Stir in vinegar. Add mushrooms, garlic, and onion. Cover skillet and cook 15 minutes. Stir. Sprinkle with parsley, and cook, uncovered, 10 minutes longer. Season with salt and pepper to taste.

Makes 2—4 servings

Nutritional Information per Serving (based on 4 servings)

Calories • 47	Calories from Fat • 13	Percent of Calories from Fat • 23%	Fat • 1.5g
Protein • 2.6g	Carbohydrate • 8g	Cholesterol • 3mg	Sodium • 16mg

6

BISCUITS AND BREADS

Light and Fluffy Biscuits

Buttermilk Biscuits

Sweet Potato Biscuits

Bran-Buttermilk Biscuits

New Orleans Luncheon Biscuits

Easy Dinner Rolls

Sweet Potato Muffins

Oatmeal Muffins

Spiced Bran Muffins

Corn Muffins

Corn Bread

Chili-Cheese Corn Bread

Hush Puppies

Dumplings

Banana Pancakes

Oatmeal Pancakes

Spicy French Toast

Apple Fritters

Biscuits and breads are the soul of southern mealtimes. Unlike traditional versions laden with fats and excessive sugars, the recipes included here demonstrate that we can still enjoy tradition while at the same time eliminating fat.

The quest for the perfect biscuit is endless among southern cooks. As a child I enjoyed the times my father was assigned the task of making the family breakfast. My father was a truck driver, and his ideal of mealtime was based on his experience of the many truckstops he encountered on his trips throughout the country. His biscuits were big enough for a giant! You only had to eat one of Daddy's hot biscuits before pulling away from the table stuffed like a teddy bear. We topped his biscuits with molasses (we called it "country syrup") and accompanied them with a tall glass of cold milk.

In these pages, I offer a number of variations on biscuits with reduced fat content. I think you'll enjoy these as much as the traditional ones your Mama, Grandma, or Daddy made.

LIGHT AND FLUFFY BISCUITS

Nonstick cooking spray
4½ cups all-purpose flour
½ cup sugar
4 teaspoons baking powder
2 teaspoons salt

¼ cup vegetable shortening
1¼ cups evaporated skim milk
¼ cup fat-free sour cream
1 egg
3 egg whites

Preheat oven to 400°F. Thoroughly coat an 8″ × 12″ pan with cooking spray. In a large mixing bowl, combine flour, sugar, baking powder, and salt. Cut the shortening into the dry ingredients. Make a well in the center of the dry ingredients, and add the milk, sour cream, egg, and egg whites. Mix wet ingredients together with a fork. Using your hands, mix dry and wet ingredients together. Dough should be soft but not sticky. (Add flour if dough is too wet, and stop mixing if dough becomes too dry.)

Transfer dough to a lightly floured surface, and roll out to a ½-inch thickness. Using a biscuit cutter (or a jar top), cut into 3½-inch rounds. Arrange in a large baking pan with biscuits touching. Re-form leftover dough to cut additional biscuits. Let biscuits stand 15 minutes in a warm place. Bake until golden brown and they spring back when touched (15 minutes on the bottom oven rack and 5 minutes on the top rack). Rotate pan if some are baking faster than others.

Makes 18 biscuits

Nutritional Information per Serving (based on 18 servings)

Calories • 183	Calories from Fat • 30	Percent of Calories from Fat • 16%	Fat • 3.3g
Protein • 5.7g	Carbohydrate • 32g	Cholesterol • 14mg	Sodium • 346mg

BUTTERMILK BISCUITS

Nonstick cooking spray
2 cups self-rising flour
1 teaspoon baking soda
2 tablespoons vegetable
  shortening

¼ cup fat-free sour cream
1 cup fat-free buttermilk

Preheat oven to 400°F. Coat a cookie sheet or jelly roll pan with cooking spray. In a medium bowl, sift flour and baking soda together. In another bowl, combine shortening, sour cream, and buttermilk. Stir into flour mixture until a soft dough forms. Transfer to a well-floured board and knead until smooth. Dough should be firm but not sticky. (Add more flour, if necessary, 1 tablespoon at a time.) Roll out ½-inch thick, and cut with a floured 2-inch round cutter. Place biscuits side-by-side on baking pan. Bake for 15 to 20 minutes, until biscuits are a deep, golden brown. Serve hot.

Makes 1 dozen biscuits

Nutritional Information per Serving (based on 12 servings)

Calories • 102	Calories from Fat • 20	Percent of Calories from Fat • 20%	Fat • 2.2g
Protein • 3.1g	Carbohydrate • 16.9g	Cholesterol • 1mg	Sodium • 394mg

SWEET POTATO BISCUITS

Nonstick cooking spray
1½ cups mashed cooked sweet
  potatoes
2 tablespoons butter, melted

½ cup evaporated skim milk
1¼ cups self-rising flour
1 tablespoon sugar
¼ teaspoon ground cinnamon

Preheat oven to 400°F. Coat a cookie sheet with cooking spray. In a large bowl, blend sweet potatoes with melted butter and evaporated milk. Mix dry ingredients in another bowl, then combine with the potato mixture, and mix well. On a floured surface, roll dough out to a ½-inch thickness, and cut with a 3-inch round cutter. Place biscuits on cookie sheet, about 1 inch apart, and bake for 20 to 25 minutes.

Makes 1 dozen biscuits

Nutritional Information per Serving (based on 12 servings)

Calories • 118	Calories from Fat • 20	Percent of Calories from Fat • 16%	Fat • 2.2g
Protein • 2.8g	Carbohydrate • 21.9g	Cholesterol • 5mg	Sodium • 202mg

BRAN-BUTTERMILK BISCUITS

Nonstick cooking spray
2 tablespoons margarine
2/3 cup self-rising flour

1/4 cup crushed bran flakes cereal
1/4 cup plus 3 tablespoons fat-free
  buttermilk

Preheat oven to 400°F. Coat a cookie sheet with nonstick cooking spray. In a medium bowl, cut margarine into flour using a pastry blender until mixture resembles coarse meal. Set aside. In a small bowl, combine bran flakes and buttermilk, and let stand 2 minutes. Add cereal mixture to flour mixture, and stir until evenly moist.

Turn dough onto a lightly floured surface and knead 5 times. Roll out to a 1/2-inch thickness, and cut out biscuits with a 2-inch cutter. Arrange biscuits on baking sheet, and bake for 15 minutes or until golden brown.

These are especially good served for breakfast with a bowl of Southern Morning Fruit Salad (see Index).

Makes 6 biscuits

Nutritional Information per Serving (based on 6 servings)

Calories • 116	Calories from Fat • 37	Percent of Calories from Fat • 31%	Fat • 4g
Protein • 3.1g	Carbohydrate • 17.7g	Cholesterol • 0mg	Sodium • 317mg

New Orleans Luncheon Biscuits

Nonstick cooking spray
3 cups all-purpose flour
2 teaspoons baking powder
1½ teaspoons salt
2 teaspoons sugar

¼ cup vegetable shortening
1¼ cups evaporated skim milk
¼ cup fat-free sour cream
¾ teaspoon fresh lemon juice

Preheat oven to 400°F. Coat two baking sheets with cooking spray. In a medium bowl, combine flour, baking powder, salt, and sugar with a fork. Using a pastry cutter, cut shortening into flour mixture until it resembles coarse cornmeal. Add 1 cup of the milk, sour cream, and lemon juice. Using a wooden spoon, gently stir mixture until the flour is moist and the dough is slightly sticky. (Stir in remaining milk, if needed, 1 tablespoon at a time.)

Turn dough out onto a floured surface. Pat dough down, and roll out to ½-inch thickness. Using a 2-inch biscuit cutter, cut out biscuits, and arrange on baking sheets. Bake on middle oven rack until golden brown and light to the touch, about 10 to 15 minutes.

Makes 30 biscuits

Nutritional Information per Serving (based on 30 servings)

Calories • 64	Calories from Fat • 16	Percent of Calories from Fat • 25%	Fat • 1.7g
Protein • 1.5g	Carbohydrate • 10.2g	Cholesterol • 0mg	Sodium • 131mg

EASY DINNER ROLLS

Nonstick cooking spray
2 cups self-rising flour
2 tablespoons sugar

1 cup evaporated skim milk
¼ cup fat-free sour cream

Heat oven to 425°F. Coat 12 muffin cups lightly with cooking spray. Combine flour and sugar in a medium bowl; set aside. Combine milk and sour cream, then add to dry mixture, and stir until moistened. Divide dough equally among muffin cups. Bake 20 minutes. Serve warm.

Makes 1 dozen rolls

Nutritional Information per Serving (based on 12 servings)

Calories • 101	Calories from Fat • 2	Percent of Calories from Fat • 2%	Fat • 0.2g
Protein • 4.0g	Carbohydrate • 20.4g	Cholesterol • 1mg	Sodium • 292mg

SWEET POTATO MUFFINS

Nonstick cooking spray
2 cups mashed cooked sweet
   potatoes
¾ cup sugar
¼ cup margarine, softened
½ cup fat–free sour cream
½ cup cholesterol–free egg
   substitute

1 cup evaporated skim milk
1½ cups all–purpose flour
3 teaspoons baking powder
1 teaspoon ground cinnamon
½ teaspoon ground nutmeg
¼ teaspoon ground cloves
¼ teaspoon salt
½ cup raisins

FAT IN BAKED GOODS

Fat performs three functions in baked goods:

1. Fat prevents the formation of tough, elastic sheets of gluten.

2. Fat holds air bubbles that help to leaven the batter.

3. Believe it or not, fat adds taste. To get the flavor lost by not using fat, substitute ingredients such as buttermilk, fruit, and purees.

To intensify flavor in muffins and other baked goods, try adding ingredients such as lemon, lime, or orange zest, or use extra shredded carrots, raisins, and spices.

Preheat oven to 400°F. Lightly spray the insides of 16 paper baking cups. Insert baking cups into muffin pans. In a large mixing bowl, mix potatoes with sugar, margarine, and sour cream. Add egg substitute and evaporated milk. Mix well. Combine flour, baking powder, cinnamon, nutmeg, cloves, and salt in a separate bowl. Add to potato mixture, and mix until smooth. Fold in raisins. Fill muffin cups to the top, and bake 25 to 30 minutes, until tops are rounded and muffins pull away from the sides of the cups.

Makes 16 muffins

Nutritional Information per Serving (based on 16 servings)

Calories • 182	Calories from Fat • 28	Percent of Calories from Fat • 15%	Fat • 3.1g
Protein • 4.4g	Carbohydrate • 34.9g	Cholesterol • 1mg	Sodium • 170mg

OATMEAL MUFFINS

Nonstick cooking spray

2 egg whites

⅓ cup pancake syrup

3 tablespoons fresh orange juice

1 cup 1% low-fat milk

1 tablespoon vanilla

1 teaspoon ground cinnamon

1 teaspoon ground allspice

1 teaspoon ground nutmeg

1½ tablespoons orange zest

1½ cups old-fashioned rolled oats
  (*not* quick-cooking)

1 cup whole-wheat flour

1 teaspoon baking powder

½ cup raisins

Preheat oven to 350°F. Coat 12 muffin cups with cooking spray. In a large mixing bowl, whisk egg whites until frothy. Whisk in the syrup, orange juice, milk, vanilla, cinnamon, allspice, nutmeg, and orange zest. With a wooden spoon, stir in oats, flour, and baking powder. Fold in raisins. Fill muffin cups two-thirds full. Bake 20 minutes or until muffins are firm in the center.

Makes 1 dozen muffins

Nutritional Information per Serving (based on 12 servings)

Calories • 136	Calories from Fat • 10	Percent of Calories from Fat • 7%	Fat • 1.2g
Protein • 4.5g	Carbohydrate • 27.8g	Cholesterol • 1mg	Sodium • 56mg

SPICED BRAN MUFFINS

Nonstick cooking spray
½ cup molasses
2 tablespoons honey
2 egg whites
¼ cup nonfat plain yogurt
¼ cup 1% low–fat milk
1 cup whole–wheat flour

½ cup wheat bran
1½ teaspoons baking powder
1 tablespoon ground ginger
½ teaspoon ground cloves
⅛ teaspoon cayenne
¾ cup raisins

Preheat oven to 350°F. Coat 12 muffin cups with cooking spray. In a small saucepan, combine molasses and honey, and heat over low heat until mixture begins to steam. Remove from heat and allow to cool.

In a large bowl, whisk together egg whites, yogurt, and milk. Whisk in cooled molasses mixture. In a separate bowl, blend together flour, bran, baking powder, ginger, cloves, cayenne, and raisins. Add dry mixture to wet mixture, and mix thoroughly with a wooden spoon. Fill muffin cups two–thirds full. Bake 15 to 20 minutes or until toothpick inserted into the center of a muffin comes out clean. Serve warm.

Makes 1 dozen muffins

Nutritional Information per Serving (based on 12 servings)

Calories • 116	Calories from Fat • 4	Percent of Calories from Fat • 3%	Fat • 0.5g
Protein • 3.1g	Carbohydrate • 27.6g	Cholesterol • 1mg	Sodium • 72mg

CORN MUFFINS

Butter-flavored nonstick cooking spray
1 cup all-purpose flour
1 cup fine yellow cornmeal
2 tablespoons sugar
1 tablespoon baking powder
1 teaspoon salt
1 egg
1 cup skim milk
2 tablespoons vegetable oil
¼ cup fat-free sour cream

Heat oven to 425°F. Lightly coat 12 muffin cups with cooking spray. Combine flour, cornmeal, sugar, baking powder, and salt in a large bowl. In a separate bowl, beat together egg, milk, oil, and sour cream. Add to flour mixture and beat with large spoon until smooth. Fill muffin cups three-quarters full. Bake 15 to 20 minutes or until lightly browned. Remove from oven and spray lightly with cooking spray. Return to oven and bake 1 minute longer. Serve warm.

Makes 1 dozen muffins

Nutritional Information per Serving (based on 12 servings)

Calories • 120	Calories from Fat • 29	Percent of Calories from Fat • 24%	Fat • 3.2g
Protein • 3.4g	Carbohydrate • 19.6g	Cholesterol • 18mg	Sodium • 283mg

Corn Bread

Nonstick cooking spray
1⅓ cups fine yellow cornmeal
1 cup all-purpose flour
3 tablespoons sugar
1 tablespoon baking powder
¼ teaspoon salt

1 cup evaporated skim milk
2 tablespoons vegetable oil
3 egg whites (or ½ cup cholesterol-free egg substitute)
½ cup low-fat plain yogurt

CORN BREAD

Corn bread is to African-American cooking as sauces are to French cooking. One of my mom's favorite treats was to have a large, cold glass of buttermilk and to crumble her corn bread into the milk and eat this by the spoonful.

Preheat oven to 375°F. Coat an 8″ × 11″ baking pan with cooking spray. In a large bowl, blend together cornmeal, flour, sugar, baking powder, and salt. In a separate bowl, beat together evaporated milk, oil, egg whites, and yogurt until blended. Make a well in the center of the flour mixture, and pour in wet ingredients. Blend well with a fork. Pour batter into baking pan, and bake on center oven rack until golden brown, about 35 minutes. Cool 5 to 10 minutes before cutting and serving.

Makes 8 servings

Nutritional Information per Serving (based on 8 servings)

Calories • 221	Calories from Fat • 41	Percent of Calories from Fat • 19%	Fat • 4.6g
Protein • 7.7g	Carbohydrate • 37.3g	Cholesterol • 2mg	Sodium • 265mg

CHILI-CHEESE CORN BREAD

Nonstick cooking spray
1 cup fine yellow cornmeal
2/3 cup all-purpose flour
2 teaspoons baking powder
1/2 teaspoon chili powder
1/2 teaspoon salt
1 cup fat-free sour cream

1 egg
1½ cups shredded fat-free
    cheddar cheese
4 ounces fresh or canned whole-
    kernel corn, drained
1 4-ounce can chopped green
    chiles, drained

Preheat oven to 400°F. Coat a 9-inch-square baking pan with cooking spray. Combine cornmeal, flour, baking powder, chili powder, and salt in a medium bowl. In a small bowl, blend sour cream and egg. Add to cornmeal mixture along with cheese, corn, and green chiles. Blend well. Pour batter into pan, and bake for 30 to 35 minutes or until toothpick inserted in center comes out clean. Cool 10 to 15 minutes before cutting and serving.

Makes 9 servings

Nutritional Information per Serving (based on 9 servings)

Calories • 150	Calories from Fat • 11	Percent of Calories from Fat • 7%	Fat • 1.2g
Protein • 10.8g	Carbohydrate • 24.7g	Cholesterol • 24mg	Sodium • 402mg

HUSH PUPPIES

1 cup white cornmeal
1 cup sifted all-purpose flour
1 teaspoon baking soda
2 teaspoons baking powder
1 teaspoon salt

½ medium yellow onion,
   chopped fine (½ cup)
1½ cups fat-free buttermilk
4 egg whites
2—6 tablespoons vegetable oil

In a large bowl, mix together cornmeal, flour, baking soda, baking powder, salt, and onion. Set aside. In a small bowl, stir together buttermilk and egg white. Mix well, and add to cornmeal mixture.

    In a heavy skillet, heat 2 tablespoons of the oil until hot. Drop batter by tablespoonfuls into the hot skillet, and cook, turning with a spatula, until hush puppies are golden brown on all sides. Repeat until all of the batter is used, adding more oil, 2 tablespoons at a time, as needed.

Makes 10—12 hush puppies (4 servings)

Nutritional Information per Serving (based on 4 servings)

Calories • 343	Calories from Fat • 76	Percent of Calories from Fat • 22%	Fat • 8.4g
Protein • 12.6g	Carbohydrate • 54.3g	Cholesterol • 2mg	Sodium • 1,175mg

DUMPLINGS

1 cup all-purpose flour
2 teaspoons baking powder
½ teaspoon salt
2 tablespoons chopped fresh
  parsley

3 egg whites
⅓ cup 1% low-fat milk
2 tablespoons margarine, melted

Prepare dumplings about 25 minutes before you need them. In a medium bowl, stir together flour, baking powder, salt, and parsley. In a small bowl, mix together egg whites, milk, and margarine. Add to flour mixture, and stir until just blended. Using a tablespoon, drop dumpling batter into the dish you are cooking. Follow recipe of main dish to determine cooking time, usually 10 to 15 minutes.

Makes 4–6 servings

Nutritional Information per Serving (based on 6 servings)

Calories • 125	Calories from Fat • 37	Percent of Calories from Fat • 30%	Fat • 4.1g
Protein • 4.4g	Carbohydrate • 17.2g	Cholesterol • 1mg	Sodium • 367mg

BANANA PANCAKES

1¼ cups all–purpose flour

½ teaspoon salt

2 tablespoons sugar

2 teaspoons baking powder

2 egg whites, lightly beaten

1½ teaspoons vegetable oil

1¼ cups skim milk

¼ teaspoon vanilla

1 medium banana, sliced thin

Nonstick cooking spray

In a large bowl, sift together flour, salt, sugar, and baking powder. In a small bowl, mix together egg whites, oil, milk, and vanilla. Add wet ingredients to dry, and blend with a fork. Add banana to batter, and stir gently. Spray a large nonstick pan or griddle with cooking spray, and heat over medium heat. For each pancake, pour ¼ cup of the batter onto the hot griddle. Turn pancakes when edges become dry and air bubbles form on the surface. Cook the other side for 2 minutes, or until golden brown.

Makes 8—10 pancakes

Nutritional Information per Serving (based on 10 servings)

Calories • 98	Calories from Fat • 8	Percent of Calories from Fat • 9%	Fat • 0.9g
Protein • 3.5g	Carbohydrate • 18.9g	Cholesterol • 1mg	Sodium • 200mg

OATMEAL PANCAKES

2 egg whites (or ¼ cup
   cholesterol–free egg substitute)
½ cup quick–cooking oats
¼ cup all–purpose flour
¼ cup whole–wheat flour
¾ cup fat–free buttermilk
¼ cup skim milk

1 tablespoon sugar
1 teaspoon baking powder
½ teaspoon baking soda
½ teaspoon salt
¼ teaspoon ground cinnamon
Nonstick cooking spray

In a medium bowl, beat egg whites with a hand beater until foamy. Add remaining ingredients except cooking spray, and beat until smooth.

   Coat a griddle or large skillet with cooking spray. Heat over medium heat. For each pancake, pour 3 tablespoons of batter onto hot griddle. Cook until edges are dry. Turn and cook other side.

Makes 12 pancakes

PANCAKES

Try cooking pancakes in butter-flavored vegetable cooking spray in lieu of other fats such as butter or shortening. When reducing the amount of fat in pancakes, it is important to preheat the skillet or griddle over low to medium heat. The skillet is ready when a few drops of water sprinkled on the hot surface sizzle.

Nutritional Information per Serving (based on 12 servings)

Calories • 45	Calories from Fat • 3	Percent of Calories from Fat • 6%	Fat • 0.3g
Protein • 2.4g	Carbohydrate • 8.3g	Cholesterol • 0mg	Sodium • 197mg

Spicy French Toast

½ cup skim milk
½ cup cholesterol-free egg
  substitute
3 tablespoons sifted powdered
  sugar
½ teaspoon ground cinnamon

¼ teaspoon ground cloves
½ teaspoon vanilla
Butter-flavored nonstick cooking
  spray
4 slices whole-wheat bread

In a shallow bowl wide enough to hold a slice of bread, combine milk, egg substitute, 1 tablespoon of the powdered sugar, cinnamon, cloves, and vanilla. Beat well. Coat a large skillet with cooking spray. Heat over medium heat. Dip bread slices, one at a time, into egg mixture, coating well. Drain off excess liquid, and arrange in skillet. Cook 3 to 5 minutes on each side, until lightly browned. Serve sprinkled with remaining powdered sugar.

Makes 4 servings

Nutritional Information per Serving (based on 4 servings)

Calories • 115	Calories from Fat • 12	Percent of Calories from Fat • 10%	Fat • 1.3g
Protein • 6.3g	Carbohydrate • 20.2g	Cholesterol • 1mg	Sodium • 217mg

APPLE FRITTERS

3 medium apples, peeled, cored,
  and cut into ¼-inch rings
1 cup whole-wheat flour
1 teaspoon baking powder
¼ teaspoon salt
½ teaspoon ground cinnamon

¼ cup cholesterol-free egg
  substitute
1 cup apple juice
1 tablespoon vegetable oil
Nonstick cooking spray
Powdered sugar

Blot apple rings dry with paper towel; set aside. In a medium bowl, mix together flour, baking powder, salt, and cinnamon. In a separate bowl, blend together egg substitute, juice, and oil. Add wet ingredients to dry, and mix until there are no lumps.

Spray a large nonstick skillet or griddle with cooking spray, and heat over medium heat. Dip apple slices, one at a time, into batter. Let excess batter drip off. Sauté a few at a time, being careful not to overcrowd griddle. Cook, turning once, until golden brown on both sides. Continue until all apples are cooked. Sprinkle with powdered sugar. Serve warm.

Makes 4 servings

Nutritional Information per Serving (based on 4 servings)

Calories • 224	Calories from Fat • 39	Percent of Calories from Fat • 16%	Fat • 4.3g
Protein • 5.6g	Carbohydrate • 44g	Cholesterol • 0mg	Sodium • 245mg

7

DESSERTS

Yam Casserole

Candied Sweet Potatoes

Sweet Potato Pie

Sweet Potato Casserole

Baked Sweet Potatoes

Blackberry Cobbler

Peach Cobbler

Good Old-Fashioned Apple Pie

Creole Sweet Potato Pone

Oatmeal Cookies

Banana Spice Bread

Pound Cake

Carrot Cake

Southern Honey Cake

Apple Cake

Peach Upside-Down Cake

Mixed Spice Cake

Raisin-Spice Coffee Cake

Bread Pudding

Blueberry Dumplings

A Word on Egg Yolks

Egg yolks are low in fat, yet high in cholesterol. Egg whites are both fat- and cholesterol-free.

Many baked goods can be made without using egg yolk. Cholesterol-free and reduced-cholesterol egg products are readily available.

Substitutions:

If recipe calls for	Use
1 large whole egg	2 egg whites
2 eggs	3 egg whites
3 eggs	5 egg whites
4 eggs	6 egg whites
5 eggs	8 egg whites
6 eggs	9 egg whites

Yam Casserole

7 medium sweet potatoes, well
   scrubbed
½ cup packed brown sugar
½ cup cholesterol–free egg
   substitute, beaten
1 teaspoon ground cinnamon

½ teaspoon ground nutmeg
1 12–ounce can frozen orange
   juice concentrate, thawed
½ cup raisins
Nonstick cooking spray
½ cup miniature marshmallows

Heat oven to 350°F. Boil or bake sweet potatoes in skins until they are tender. Allow to cool.

Peel and mash sweet potatoes, removing any strings. Combine sweet potatoes, sugar, egg substitute, and spices in a large bowl. Beat with hand mixer for 2 minutes, adding juice as needed to achieve a smooth consistency. Stir in raisins.

Coat a 2–quart baking dish with cooking spray. Transfer mixture to baking dish and sprinkle marshmallows over top. Bake, uncovered, for 30 minutes or until a light crust forms.

Makes 6—8 servings

Nutritional Information per Serving (based on 8 servings)

| Calories • 260 | Calories from Fat • 3 | Percent of Calories from Fat • 1% | Fat • 0.3g |
| Protein • 4.4g | Carbohydrate • 62.2g | Cholesterol • 0mg | Sodium • 44mg |

CANDIED SWEET POTATOES

Nonstick cooking spray
2 pounds sweet potatoes, peeled
   and cut into ¼-inch slices
1½ cups cold water
1 teaspoon vanilla
2 tablespoons margarine,
   softened

½ cup brown sugar
¼ cup granulated sugar
1 teaspoon ground cinnamon
½ teaspoon ground allspice
½ teaspoon ground cloves
¼ cup raisins
¼ cup canned crushed pineapple

Preheat oven to 400°F. Coat a 9″ × 12″ baking dish with cooking spray. Arrange sweet potato slices in baking dish. Combine water and vanilla, and pour over sweet potatoes. Mix the margarine, sugars, and spices in a small bowl until blended. Sprinkle sugar mixture over the sweet potatoes. Cover tightly and bake for 45 minutes.

In a small bowl, mix together raisins and pineapple with its juice, and sprinkle over the sweet potatoes. Baste with the juices from the pan. Cover and continue baking until sweet potatoes are tender and juices are bubbling, about 20 minutes.

Makes 8 servings

Nutritional Information per Serving (based on 8 servings)

Calories • 215	Calories from Fat • 28	Percent of Calories from Fat • 13%	Fat • 3.2g
Protein • 1.7g	Carbohydrate • 46.5g	Cholesterol • 0mg	Sodium • 52mg

SWEET POTATO PIE

4 medium sweet potatoes,
cooked, peeled, and mashed
(3 cups)

4 egg whites

6 ounces neufchâtel cheese, room
temperature

¼ cup sugar

¼ cup orange juice

2 tablespoons margarine

½ teaspoon ground nutmeg

½ teaspoon ground cinnamon

¼ teaspoon ground ginger

¼ teaspoon ground cloves

¼ teaspoon ground allspice

2 tablespoons vanilla

1 frozen deep-dish piecrust,
thawed

NUTMEG

Nutmeg, native to Indonesia, is most commonly used in dessert cooking. Select whole nutmegs and grate them with a small grater for the fullest flavor.

Preheat oven to 350°F. In a large bowl, combine all ingredients except the pie-crust. Mix well, and pour into unbaked piecrust. Bake for 1 hour or until center is firm but not sticky to the touch. Cool 30 minutes.

Makes 10—12 servings

Nutritional Information per Serving (based on 12 servings)

Calories • 172	Calories from Fat • 50	Percent of Calories from Fat • 29%	Fat • 5.5g
Protein • 4g	Carbohydrate • 26g	Cholesterol • 11mg	Sodium • 108mg

SWEET POTATO CASSEROLE

Nonstick cooking spray

3 cups mashed baked sweet
potatoes (4 large potatoes),
cooled

¼ cup sugar

2 teaspoons margarine

½ teaspoon lemon juice

¼ cup raisins

½ teaspoon ground ginger

¼ teaspoon ground allspice

3 egg whites

1 teaspoon vanilla

⅓ cup evaporated skim milk

Preheat oven to 350°F. Thoroughly coat a deep 2-quart casserole with cooking spray. Combine remaining ingredients in a large bowl, and mix well. Pour mixture into casserole, and bake for 25 minutes or until top is browned.

Makes 10—12 servings

Nutritional Information per Serving (based on 12 servings)

Calories • 128	Calories from Fat • 8	Percent of Calories from Fat • 6%	Fat • 0.9g
Protein • 2.9g	Carbohydrate • 27.6g	Cholesterol • 0mg	Sodium • 40mg

Baked Sweet Potatoes

6 medium sweet potatoes
Nonstick cooking spray
1½ teaspoons ground cinnamon

½ teaspoon ground nutmeg
¼ cup sugar

Preheat oven to 350°F. Scrub potatoes and pat dry. Lightly rub cooking spray onto skin of each sweet potato. With a fork, prick the surface of each sweet potato four times. Bake for 1 hour (or until a fork inserted into the potato encounters no resistance). In a small bowl, blend together cinnamon, nutmeg, and sugar. Sprinkle on sweet potatoes after cooking.

Makes 6 servings

Nutritional Information per Serving (based on 6 servings)

Calories • 152	Calories from Fat • 2	Percent of Calories from Fat • 1%	Fat • 0.2g
Protein • 2g	Carbohydrate • 36.6g	Cholesterol • 0mg	Sodium • 12mg

BLACKBERRY COBBLER

1 cup all–purpose flour
Dash salt
1 teaspoon baking powder
2 teaspoons butter
2 tablespoons fat-free sour cream

¼ cup skim milk
Nonstick cooking spray
5 cups fresh blackberries
½ cup sugar

In a large bowl, stir together flour, salt, and baking powder. Blend butter and sour cream together in a small bowl. Add to flour mixture, and slowly stir in milk. Transfer dough to a lightly floured board, and knead until smooth but not sticky. Roll out dough to ¼-inch thickness.

Preheat oven to 425°F. Spray a 9″ × 13″ glass baking dish with cooking spray. Arrange blackberries in baking dish. Sprinkle with sugar. Cut dough into 1-inch-wide strips, and arrange on top of blackberries at ¼-inch intervals in a criss-cross pattern. Bake for 30 to 40 minutes or until blackberries begin to bubble and dough is golden brown.

Makes 4—6 servings

Nutritional Information per Serving (based on 6 servings)

Calories • 219	Calories from Fat • 18	Percent of Calories from Fat • 8%	Fat • 2g
Protein • 3.5g	Carbohydrate • 48.7g	Cholesterol • 4mg	Sodium • 75mg

Peach Cobbler

Nonstick cooking spray
4 cups very ripe peaches, sliced
4 tablespoons sugar
1 tablespoon quick–cooking
   tapioca, uncooked
1 tablespoon fresh lemon juice
½ teaspoon ground cloves

1 cup self-rising flour
2 tablespoons well–chilled
   margarine
1½ tablespoons fat-free sour
   cream
5 tablespoons skim milk

Spray a 9–inch pie pan with cooking spray. In a large bowl, combine peaches, 3 tablespoons of the sugar, tapioca, lemon juice, and cloves. Transfer to pie pan, and let stand 20 minutes. In a medium bowl, combine flour and the remaining tablespoon of sugar. Cut in the margarine and sour cream with a fork until mixture resembles a coarse meal. Stir in milk to form a ball. On a lightly floured surface, roll dough out into a 10–inch circle. Place dough over fruit filling. Trim edges of dough and decorate by crimping. Chill 30 minutes.

Preheat oven to 375°F. Make small slits in the crust to allow steam to escape. Bake for 30 minutes, until the crust is golden brown and the filling is bubbly.

Makes 8 servings

Nutritional Information per Serving (based on 8 servings)

Calories • 151	Calories from Fat • 28	Percent of Calories from Fat • 18%	Fat • 3.1g
Protein • 2.7g	Carbohydrate • 29.4g	Cholesterol • 0mg	Sodium • 239mg

GOOD OLD-FASHIONED APPLE PIE

2 frozen 9-inch piecrusts, thawed
½ cup plus 2 tablespoons
  granulated sugar
½ cup firmly packed brown
  sugar
2 tablespoons all-purpose flour
½ teaspoon ground cinnamon

¼ teaspoon ground nutmeg
1 tablespoon butter-flavored
  shortening
4—5 tart baking apples, peeled
  and sliced (6 cups)
3 tablespoons apple juice
¼ cup evaporated skim milk

Preheat oven to 375°F. Arrange bottom piecrust in a pie pan. In a large bowl, combine ½ cup of the granulated sugar, brown sugar, flour, cinnamon, and nutmeg. Using a fork, cut in shortening until mixture is coarse. Toss apples into mixture, and spoon into unbaked piecrust. Sprinkle apples with apple juice. Moisten edge of crust with water.

Arrange top crust over filled shell, and trim ½ inch beyond edge of pie pan. Fold edges under. Cut slits in top crust to allow steam to escape. Brush surface with milk, and sprinkle with remaining 2 tablespoons granulated sugar. Bake for 45 to 50 minutes or until filling is bubbly and crust is golden brown.

Makes 8 servings

Nutritional Information per Serving (based on 8 servings)

Calories • 341	Calories from Fat • 109	Percent of Calories from Fat • 31%	Fat • 12.1g
Protein • 2.3g	Carbohydrate • 57.4g	Cholesterol • 0mg	Sodium • 219mg

CREOLE SWEET POTATO PONE

Nonstick cooking spray
6 raw sweet potatoes, grated
2 egg whites
¼ cup light brown sugar
½ cup molasses
2 tablespoons butter

1½ cups skim milk
1 teaspoon vanilla
1 teaspoon ground cinnamon
½ teaspoon ground nutmeg
½ teaspoon ground ginger

Preheat oven to 325°F. Coat a heavy 4- to 5-quart baking dish with cooking spray. Combine remaining ingredients in a large bowl, and mix well. Transfer to baking dish, and bake for 2½ hours. Test potatoes for tenderness (done when golden brown and bubbly).

Makes 6 servings

Nutritional Information per Serving (based on 6 servings)

Calories • 275	Calories from Fat • 37	Percent of Calories from Fat • 13%	Fat • 4.1g
Protein • 5.3g	Carbohydrate • 55.4g	Cholesterol • 11mg	Sodium • 130mg

OATMEAL COOKIES

Nonstick cooking spray
¼ cup fat-free sour cream
1 cup sugar
4 egg whites
2 cups all-purpose flour
½ teaspoon baking soda
½ teaspoon salt

½ teaspoon ground cinnamon
½ teaspoon ground cloves
¼ cup 1% low-fat milk
2 cups old-fashioned rolled oats
 (*not* quick-cooking)
1 cup raisins

Preheat oven to 375°F. Coat 2 cookie sheets with cooking spray. In a large bowl, combine sour cream, sugar, and egg whites. Beat well. Stir in flour, baking soda, salt, cinnamon, and cloves. Gradually add milk. Add oatmeal, ½ cup at a time, stirring gently. Stir in raisins, and mix dough thoroughly.

Drop by tablespoonfuls onto cookie sheets. Bake for 12 to 15 minutes. (The shorter time produces chewier cookies.)

Makes 2 dozen cookies

Nutritional Information per Serving (based on 24 servings)

Calories • 120	Calories from Fat • 1	Percent of Calories from Fat • 4%	Fat • 0.6g
Protein • 3.2g	Carbohydrate • 26g	Cholesterol • 0mg	Sodium • 84mg

Banana Spice Bread

Nonstick cooking spray
2 cups all-purpose flour
1 tablespoon baking powder
¼ teaspoon salt
½ teaspoon ground nutmeg
½ teaspoon ground cinnamon
¼ teaspoon ground cloves
⅛ teaspoon cayenne

2 large ripe bananas, peeled
1 teaspoon vanilla
3 egg whites
¼ cup nonfat vanilla yogurt
½ cup applesauce
¼ cup unsalted butter, softened
½ cup sugar
½ cup raisins

Preheat oven to 350°F. Coat a 5″ × 9″ loaf pan with cooking spray. Sift flour, baking powder, salt, and spices together in a large bowl. In another large bowl, mash bananas with vanilla until smooth. Add egg whites, yogurt, and applesauce to banana mixture, and blend well. In a small bowl, cream butter and sugar until fluffy. Set aside.

Stir half the dry ingredients into the banana mixture. Stir in butter mixture and raisins, and blend well. Add remaining dry ingredients to banana mixture and stir until smooth. Pour batter into loaf pan, and bake 1 hour, until golden brown (or toothpick comes out clean). Cool in pan.

Makes 8—10 servings

Nutritional Information per Serving (based on 10 servings)

Calories • 234	Calories from Fat • 48	Percent of Calories from Fat • 20%	Fat • 5.3g
Protein • 4.5g	Carbohydrate • 43.3g	Cholesterol • 13mg	Sodium • 175mg

POUND CAKE

Butter-flavored nonstick cooking
  spray
2 cups self-rising flour
1 cup sugar
4 egg whites

½ cup 1% low-fat milk
2 tablespoons butter, softened
¾ cup nonfat plain yogurt
¼ teaspoon ground cinnamon
1 teaspoon vanilla

Coat a 10-inch tube pan with cooking spray. Combine remaining ingredients in a large bowl, and beat for 2–5 minutes with an electric mixer. Pour batter into pan. Place pan in cold oven, then heat oven to 350°F. Bake for 1 hour or until cake is golden brown on top and it springs back when touched. Let cool 20 minutes before removing from pan.

Makes 8 servings

Nutritional Information per Serving (based on 8 servings)

Calories • 261	Calories from Fat • 30	Percent of Calories from Fat • 12%	Fat • 3.4g
Protein • 6.6g	Carbohydrate • 51g	Cholesterol • 8.7mg	Sodium • 478mg

CARROT CAKE

Nonstick cooking spray
2¼ cups all-purpose flour
1 cup sugar
2 teaspoons baking soda
1½ teaspoons ground cinnamon
½ teaspoon ground nutmeg
½ teaspoon ground cloves
½ teaspoon salt
½ cup fat-free sour cream
2 tablespoons vegetable oil
5 egg whites
¾ cup evaporated skim milk

6 carrots, shredded (2½ cups)
¼ cup finely chopped walnuts
¾ cup raisins

Cream Cheese Frosting

1 8-ounce package fat-free cream
cheese
½ cup fat-free sour cream
¼ cup evaporated skim milk
2 teaspoons vanilla
2 cups powdered sugar

Preheat oven to 325°F. Coat a 9″ × 13″ pan with cooking spray. In a large bowl, combine flour, sugar, baking soda, cinnamon, nutmeg, cloves, and salt. In a separate bowl, blend together sour cream, vegetable oil, egg whites, milk, and carrot. Add to flour mixture and beat with an electric mixer on low speed, scraping bowl constantly, until ingredients are moistened. Beat on medium speed for 2 minutes. Stir in nuts and raisins. Pour batter into pan and bake for 50 to 60 minutes, until toothpick inserted in center of cake comes out clean. Cool completely before frosting.

CREAM CHEESE FROSTING

Combine cream cheese, sour cream, milk, and vanilla in a large bowl. Beat with electric mixer on medium speed until fluffy. Gradually add powdered sugar until desired consistency is reached. Frost entire cake, or serve frosting on the side.

Makes 8—12 servings

Nutritional Information per Serving (based on 12 servings)

Calories • 250	Calories from Fat • 37	Percent of Calories from Fat • 15%	Fat • 4.1g
Protein • 6.9g	Carbohydrate • 47.6g	Cholesterol • 1mg	Sodium • 357mg

SOUTHERN HONEY CAKE

Nonstick cooking spray
2½ cups all-purpose flour
2½ teaspoons baking powder
¼ teaspoon salt
¼ teaspoon baking soda
½ teaspoon ground cinnamon
¼ teaspoon ground nutmeg
⅛ teaspoon ground cloves
1 cup fat-free sour cream

½ cup sugar
1 teaspoon vanilla
¾ cup honey
4 egg whites
1 cup hot water
¼ cup finely chopped walnuts
1 recipe Mock Whipped Cream
  (see Index)

Preheat oven to 350°F. Spray a 9″ × 13″ baking pan with cooking spray. In a medium bowl, combine flour, baking powder, salt, baking soda, cinnamon, nutmeg, and cloves. In a large bowl, blend together sour cream, sugar, vanilla, honey, and egg whites. Stir dry ingredients into wet, and slowly beat in water with an electric mixer on low speed until smooth. Spread batter in pan, and sprinkle nuts over top. Bake 30 to 35 minutes or until toothpick inserted in center comes out clean. Cool 15 minutes before serving. Serve topped with Mock Whipped Cream.

Makes 12 servings

Nutritional Information per Serving (based on 12 servings)

Calories • 227	Calories from Fat • 16	Percent of Calories from Fat • 7%	Fat • 1.8g
Protein • 5.8g	Carbohydrate • 48g	Cholesterol • 0mg	Sodium • 172mg

Apple Cake

Nonstick cooking spray

⅓ cup boiling water

2 cups chopped apple, unpeeled

1¼ cups firmly packed brown sugar

2 cups all-purpose flour

5 egg whites

⅓ cup fat-free sour cream

1 teaspoon vanilla

1¼ teaspoons baking soda

1 teaspoon ground cinnamon

½ teaspoon ground cloves

¼ teaspoon salt

1 recipe Mock Whipped Cream (see Index)

Preheat oven to 350°F. Coat a 9″ × 13″ pan with cooking spray. In a large bowl, pour boiling water over apple. Add brown sugar, flour, egg whites, sour cream, vanilla, baking soda, cinnamon, cloves, and salt. Beat with an electric mixer on low speed 1 minute, scraping bowl constantly, then beat on medium speed 3 minutes, scraping bowl occasionally. Pour batter into pan. Bake 40 to 45 minutes or until toothpick inserted in center of cake comes out clean. Serve warm with Mock Whipped Cream.

Makes 12 servings

Nutritional Information per Serving (based on 12 servings)

Calories • 199	Calories from Fat • 3	Percent of Calories from Fat • 1%	Fat • 0.3g
Protein • 5.2g	Carbohydrate • 43.8g	Cholesterol • 0mg	Sodium • 229mg

PEACH UPSIDE-DOWN CAKE

1 tablespoon butter, melted
½ cup firmly packed brown
  sugar
½ teaspoon ground cinnamon
¼ teaspoon ground nutmeg
2 cups fresh sliced peaches
½ cup fat-free sour cream

⅔ cup sugar
½ cup skim milk
3 egg whites
1 teaspoon vanilla
1½ cups all-purpose flour
1½ teaspoons baking powder
½ teaspoon salt

Preheat oven to 350°F. Coat a 9-inch square baking pan with melted butter. Mix together brown sugar, cinnamon, and nutmeg in a small bowl. Sprinkle evenly on top of melted butter. Arrange peaches on top of sugar mixture.

In a large bowl, beat together sour cream, sugar, and milk until light and fluffy. Blend in egg whites and vanilla. In a medium bowl, stir together flour, baking powder, and salt. Add to batter, and mix well. Spread batter over fruit. Bake for 1 hour or until toothpick inserted in center of cake comes out clean. Allow to cool in pan. Invert cake onto platter to serve.

Makes 8 servings

Nutritional Information per Serving (based on 8 servings)

Calories • 256	Calories from Fat • 16	Percent of Calories from Fat • 6%	Fat • 1.7g
Protein • 5.5g	Carbohydrate • 55.4g	Cholesterol • 4mg	Sodium • 253mg

Mixed Spice Cake

Nonstick cooking spray
½ cup golden raisins
½ cup orange juice
2¼ cups self-rising flour
¼ cup firmly packed brown
   sugar
2 teaspoons poppy seed
½ teaspoon ground cinnamon

½ teaspoon ground allspice
¼ teaspoon ground ginger
⅛ teaspoon cayenne
1¼ cups fat-free buttermilk
3 egg whites
½ cup unsweetened applesauce
1 teaspoon vanilla
Powdered sugar

Preheat oven to 350°F. Coat a 9″ × 13″ pan with cooking spray. In a small bowl, soak raisins in orange juice for 15 minutes. In a large bowl, mix together flour, brown sugar, poppy seed, cinnamon, allspice, ginger, and cayenne. Stir in raisin mixture, buttermilk, egg whites, applesauce, and vanilla.

Pour batter into pan. Bake 35 to 40 minutes or until toothpick inserted in center of cake comes out clean. Cool cake completely, then dust with powdered sugar.

Makes 12 servings

Nutritional Information per Serving (based on 12 servings)

Calories • 147	Calories from Fat • 5	Percent of Calories from Fat • 3%	Fat • 0.5g
Protein • 4.5g	Carbohydrate • 31.3g	Cholesterol • 0mg	Sodium • 341mg

RAISIN-SPICE COFFEE CAKE

Nonstick cooking spray
1 cup whole-wheat flour
¾ cup firmly packed brown
   sugar
2 tablespoons margarine
1 cup skim milk
¼ cup fat-free sour cream
1 tablespoon baking powder

1 teaspoon ground cinnamon
½ teaspoon salt
¼ teaspoon ground allspice
¼ teaspoon ground nutmeg
4 egg whites (or ½ cup
   cholesterol-free egg substitute)
¾ cup raisins

Preheat oven to 350°F. Coat a 9-inch square pan with cooking spray. Combine all ingredients except raisins in a large bowl. Beat with an electric mixer on medium speed 3 minutes, scraping bowl occasionally. Stir in raisins, and spread batter in pan. Bake 40 to 45 minutes or until toothpick inserted in center of cake comes out clean. Serve warm.

Makes 8 servings

Nutritional Information per Serving (based on 8 servings)

Calories • 221	Calories from Fat • 29	Percent of Calories from Fat • 13%	Fat • 3.3g
Protein • 5.8g	Carbohydrate • 44.8g	Cholesterol • 1mg	Sodium • 348mg

BREAD PUDDING

2 cups skim milk

2 cups evaporated skim milk

12 cups day-old French bread or bread cubes

1 28-ounce can peach halves packed in juice, drained and cut into large chunks

1 cup raisins

2 tablespoons margarine, melted

6 egg whites

½ cup firmly packed brown sugar

¼ cup granulated sugar

1 teaspoon vanilla

1½ teaspoons ground cinnamon

¾ teaspoon ground nutmeg

¼ teaspoon ground allspice

½ teaspoon salt

Butter-flavored nonstick cooking spray

BREAD PUDDING

There was nothing better than Miss Sophia's bread pudding. All the neighborhood kids loved the smell of cinnamon and nutmeg. Keep in mind that the bread you use should be dry and slightly hard. This will give the pudding its chewy texture when baked.

Preheat oven to 350°F. In a large bowl, combine skim milk with evaporated milk. Soak bread for 20 minutes, adding additional milk if mixture is too dry. Stir in peaches, raisins, and margarine. Mix thoroughly.

In a separate bowl beat together egg whites, sugars, vanilla, cinnamon, nutmeg, all-spice, and salt until thoroughly blended. Combine with bread mixture, and blend well.

Thoroughly coat a 3- to 4-quart casserole with cooking spray. Pour mixture into casserole, making sure that ingredients are well distributed. Bake for 1 hour or until knife inserted in center comes out clean. (Top should be brown with a rough crust.)

Serve warm or chilled, with Bourbon Raisin Sauce, Mock Whipped Cream, or Creamy Cinnamon Sauce (see Index).

Makes 8—10 servings

Nutritional Information per Serving (based on 10 servings)

Calories • 326	Calories from Fat • 36	Percent of Calories from Fat • 11%	Fat • 4g
Protein • 11.6g	Carbohydrate • 62.8g	Cholesterol • 2mg	Sodium • 445mg

BLUEBERRY DUMPLINGS

3 pints fresh blueberries, washed
   and sorted

2 quarts water

2 cups sugar

Dumplings

1 cup all-purpose flour

1 cup whole-wheat flour

1 tablespoon baking powder

½ teaspoon salt

1 cup evaporated skim milk

Combine blueberries, water, and sugar in a 5-quart pot. Bring to a boil over medium heat. Boil for 5 minutes, then reduce heat to simmer.

DUMPLINGS

In a large bowl, sift together all-purpose flour, whole-wheat flour, baking powder, and salt. Make a well in the center of the dry ingredients, and slowly pour in evaporated milk while stirring gently with a fork. Dough should be semisoft. *Do not overmix.*

   Gently form dough into pecan-sized balls. Lower dumplings gently into the simmering berry liquid. Cover and simmer until toothpick inserted into the center of a dumpling comes out clean, about 20 to 25 minutes.

Serve with vanilla frozen yogurt or Mock Whipped Cream (see Index).

Makes 8 servings

Nutritional Information per Serving (based on 8 servings)

Calories • 388	Calories from Fat • 8	Percent of Calories from Fat • 2%	Fat • 0.9g
Protein • 6.8g	Carbohydrate • 92.2g	Cholesterol • 1mg	Sodium • 309mg

8

Seasoning Blends, Dressings, Sauces, and Toppings

Salt-Free Cajun Seasoning Blend

Louisiana Seasoning Mix

Cajun Spice Mix

Southern Salsa

Cajun Roux

Chicken Gravy

Ginger Garlic Sauce

Dilled Mustard Sauce

Creamy Cinnamon Sauce

Bourbon Raisin Sauce (with Turkey)

Low-Fat Chocolate Sauce

Apple-Blueberry Syrup

Mock Whipped Cream

Raisin Spread

SALT-FREE CAJUN SEASONING BLEND

¼ cup plus 2 tablespoons onion
    powder
1 tablespoon garlic powder
3 tablespoons poultry seasoning

3 tablespoons sweet paprika
2 tablespoons dry mustard
2 teaspoons ground oregano
1 teaspoon cayenne

Blend ingredients together thoroughly and store in an airtight container
for at least 24 hours before using. Pour into a shaker and use to season
meat, poultry, or vegetable dishes.

Makes about 1 cup (1 teaspoon per serving)

Nutritional Information per Serving (based on 48 servings)

Calories • 7	Calories from Fat • 2	Percent of Calories from Fat • 21%	Fat • 0.2g
Protein • 0.3g	Carbohydrate • 1.3g	Cholesterol • 0mg	Sodium • 1mg

Louisiana Seasoning Mix

1½ tablespoons paprika

1½ tablespoons dried thyme

1 tablespoon dried basil

1 tablespoon dried oregano

½ teaspoon cayenne

¼ teaspoon black pepper

1 teaspoon garlic powder

1 bay leaf

Place all ingredients in a blender and grind until well blended. Use whenever Cajun or Creole seasoning mix is called for.

Makes about ¼ cup (1 teaspoon per serving)

Nutritional Information per Serving (based on 12 servings)

Calories • 7	Calories from Fat • 2	Percent of Calories from Fat • 21%	Fat • 0.2g
Protein • 0.3g	Carbohydrate • 1.5g	Cholesterol • 0mg	Sodium • 1mg

CAJUN SPICE MIX

½ cup sweet paprika

2 tablespoons cayenne

2 tablespoons freshly ground
   black pepper

1 tablespoon dried oregano

1 tablespoon dried thyme

1 tablespoon onion powder

2 teaspoons reduced-sodium
   table salt

1½ teaspoons celery seed

¾ teaspoon garlic powder

Place all ingredients in a blender and grind until well blended.

Makes about 1 cup (1 teaspoon per serving)

Nutritional Information per Serving (based on 48 servings)

Calories • 6	Calories from Fat • 2	Percent of Calories from Fat • 25%	Fat • 0.2g
Protein • 0.3g	Carbohydrate • 1.2g	Cholesterol • 0mg	Sodium • 47mg

Southern Salsa

3 medium ripe tomatoes, chopped coarse

1 medium red bell pepper, chopped coarse

½ medium green bell pepper, chopped coarse

1 medium onion, diced coarse

4 cloves garlic, chopped coarse

2 jalapeño peppers, seeded and cut into thin pieces

Juice from ½ lime

2 tablespoons white distilled vinegar

1 teaspoon Tabasco

Chill a medium serving bowl. Place all ingredients in a food processor and process on low speed for 10 seconds. Pour into chilled bowl. Serve with fat-free sour cream over your favorite seafood dish or on top of baked potatoes.

Makes 1½ cups salsa

Nutritional Information per Serving (based on 2 servings)

Calories • 129	Calories from Fat • 11	Percent of Calories from Fat • 7%	Fat • 1.2g
Protein • 4.9g	Carbohydrate • 29.3g	Cholesterol • 0mg	Sodium • 98mg

CAJUN ROUX

¼ cup vegetable oil   1 cup all–purpose flour

Heat oil in a cast iron dutch oven or 12–inch skillet over medium heat. When oil is hot, add flour, a little at a time, and stir quickly to blend and prevent lumps. Reduce heat to medium–low. Cook, stirring constantly, until roux browns to desired color (peanut to mahogany). If roux burns, discard it and start over, or the dish you use it in will be ruined.

To stop cooking, add roux to recipe or stir in a metal bowl until it cools, to prevent separation. Roux may be refrigerated for up to one week or frozen for up to six months.

Makes ⅔ cup

ROUX

Roux is the sauce that makes many southern dishes unique. This thickening agent is used in gumbos and stews (this book reduces the typical amounts of fat used to produce a roux without diminishing the taste of the dish). Properly prepared, roux is completely absorbed into a dish, but the taste and texture are an essential part of southern cooking.

This recipe cuts the fat by 75 percent; however, it takes a watchful eye not to let the roux burn. The cooking is a lot quicker, and therefore reduced-fat roux can burn fast if you don't keep an eye on it. Constant stirring is a MUST!

Nutritional Information per Serving (based on 6 servings)

Calories • 156	Calories from Fat • 84	Percent of Calories from Fat • 54%	Fat • 9.3g
Protein • 2.2g	Carbohydrate • 15.9g	Cholesterol • 0mg	Sodium • 0mg

Chicken Gravy

1 cup Chicken Broth (see Index)
2 tablespoons flour
¼ cup evaporated skim milk

½ teaspoon freshly ground black
   pepper, or to taste

Warm chicken broth in a saucepan over medium heat. Place flour and milk in a small bowl and whisk until smooth (or place in a jar with a tight-fitting lid and shake until smooth). Gradually stir milk mixture into chicken broth and cook over medium heat, stirring constantly, until thick. Add pepper, reduce heat, and continue to cook, stirring constantly, until mixture becomes thick, about 5 minutes.

Makes 1 cup gravy

Nutritional Information per Serving (based on 2 servings)

Calories • 67	Calories from Fat • 5	Percent of Calories from Fat • 8%	Fat • 0.6g
Protein • 4.9g	Carbohydrate • 10.4g	Cholesterol • 6mg	Sodium • 48mg

GINGER GARLIC SAUCE

1 teaspoon canola oil
¼ cup sliced scallion
½ teaspoon grated fresh ginger
1 clove garlic, minced

½ cup cold water
1½ teaspoons cornstarch
1 teaspoon low-sodium soy sauce

In a small saucepan, heat oil over medium heat. Add scallion, ginger, and garlic and sauté for 1 minute. In a small bowl, stir together water, cornstarch, and soy sauce. Add to saucepan and cook, stirring, over medium heat until mixture is thick and bubbly. Serve hot over meat or seafood and cooked rice.

Makes ⅔ cup sauce

Nutritional Information per Serving (based on 2 servings)

Calories • 34	Calories from Fat • 21	Percent of Calories from Fat • 59%	Fat • 2.2g
Protein • 0.5g	Carbohydrate • 3.1g	Cholesterol • 0mg	Sodium • 91mg

DILLED MUSTARD SAUCE

1 cup nonfat plain yogurt
2 tablespoons Dijon mustard
1 teaspoon chopped fresh chives

1 teaspoon fresh lemon juice
½ teaspoon dried whole dill

Combine all ingredients in a small bowl; mix well. Cover and chill. Serve with chicken, fish, or vegetables.

Makes 1 cup sauce

Nutritional Information per Serving (based on 2 servings)

Calories • 79	Calories from Fat • 11	Percent of Calories from Fat • 13%	Fat • 1.2g
Protein • 7.5g	Carbohydrate • 9.9g	Cholesterol • 2mg	Sodium • 289mg

CREAMY CINNAMON SAUCE

1 cup nonfat vanilla yogurt
½ cup fat-free cottage cheese
1 tablespoon firmly packed
  brown sugar

½ teaspoon ground cinnamon
½ teaspoon vanilla

Combine all ingredients in a blender or food processor. Process until smooth. Chill thoroughly. Serve over fresh fruit or angel food cake. Store in a covered container in the refrigerator for up to one week.

Makes 1½ cups sauce

Nutritional Information per Serving (based on 6 servings)

Calories • 52	Calories from Fat • 0	Percent of Calories from Fat • 0%	Fat • 0g
Protein • 4.3g	Carbohydrate • 8.8g	Cholesterol • 0mg	Sodium • 74mg

Bourbon Raisin Sauce (with Turkey)

Nonstick cooking spray
1 teaspoon margarine
4 pounds smoked turkey thighs, deboned and cut into ¼-inch-thick pieces

Sauce
1½ tablespoons cornstarch
1 cup apple cider
½ teaspoon ground allspice
2 teaspoons fresh lemon juice
2 tablespoons bourbon
¼ cup raisins
Pinch salt

ALLSPICE

Allspice, which tastes like a combination of cinnamon and nutmeg (hence its name), comes from the underripe berry of a tropical evergreen tree. Ground allspice is frequently used in southern recipes.

Coat a large skillet with cooking spray and melt margarine over medium heat. Add turkey to skillet and cook about 3 minutes per side. Remove from skillet and keep warm.

In a small bowl, blend cornstarch with 6 tablespoons of the apple cider; set aside. Deglaze skillet with remaining cider, then stir in allspice and lemon juice. Stirring constantly, add the cornstarch mixture and bring to a boil. Cook, stirring constantly, until sauce becomes thick. Add bourbon, raisins, and salt, and cook 5 minutes longer. Serve over turkey thighs.

Makes 4—8 servings

Nutritional Information per Serving (based on 8 servings)

Calories • 440	Calories from Fat • 240	Percent of Calories from Fat • 54%	Fat • 26.7g
Protein • 28.5g	Carbohydrate • 20.3g	Cholesterol • 0mg	Sodium • 1,793mg

LOW-FAT CHOCOLATE SAUCE

½ cup sugar
3 tablespoons evaporated skim
  milk

1 tablespoon unsweetened cocoa
1 tablespoon light corn syrup
1 teaspoon vanilla

In a saucepan, combine sugar, milk, cocoa, and corn syrup. Bring to a boil. Boil for 1 minute, then remove from heat and stir in vanilla. Serve immediately over angel food cake or the dessert of your choice.

Makes ⅓ cup sauce

Nutritional Information per Serving (based on 2 servings)

Calories • 254	Calories from Fat • 3	Percent of Calories from Fat • 1%	Fat • 0.3g
Protein • 2.3g	Carbohydrate • 62.5g	Cholesterol • 1mg	Sodium • 38mg

Apple-Blueberry Syrup

½ cup frozen apple juice
concentrate, thawed
2 teaspoons sugar
1½ tablespoons cornstarch
1 cup boiling water

1 16-ounce package frozen
blueberries, thawed and
drained
1 tablespoon fresh lemon juice

Combine apple juice, sugar, and cornstarch in a saucepan. Stir until well blended. Add boiling water, and cook over medium heat, stirring constantly, until mixture comes to a full boil. Stir in blueberries and lemon juice. Reduce heat and simmer for 3 minutes, stirring constantly. Serve warm or chilled over pancakes, biscuits, or plain cakes.

Makes 2 cups syrup

Nutritional Information per Serving (based on 6 servings)

Calories • 91	Calories from Fat • 5	Percent of Calories from Fat • 5%	Fat • 0.6g
Protein • 0.5g	Carbohydrate • 22.3g	Cholesterol • 0mg	Sodium • 8mg

MOCK WHIPPED CREAM

1 can evaporated skim milk,
   chilled

1 teaspoon vanilla
1 teaspoon brandy

Chill a medium stainless–steel bowl and electric beaters for 2 hours. Pour chilled evaporated milk into chilled bowl. Add vanilla and brandy. Beat at high speed until peaks form. Use immediately.

Makes 2 cups

Nutritional Information per Serving (based on 6 servings)

Calories • 26	Calories from Fat • 0.5	Percent of Calories from Fat • 2%	Fat • 0.1g
Protein • 2.1g	Carbohydrate • 3.5g	Cholesterol • 1mg	Sodium • 33mg

Raisin Spread

1 cup golden raisins

1 cup cold water

¼ cup unsweetened applesauce

¼ teaspoon ground allspice

½ teaspoon finely grated lemon rind

1 teaspoon fresh lemon juice

In a 1½–quart saucepan, combine raisins with water. Cover pan and bring to a boil over high heat. When raisins become plump, about 30 minutes, transfer to a strainer and rinse under cold water. Set strainer over a bowl. With the back of a wooden spoon, squeeze excess liquid from raisins. Discard liquid.

Place raisins and remaining ingredients in a blender or food processor (with metal blade). Process, scraping sides occasionally, until a smooth paste forms. Refrigerate for 2 to 4 hours. Store in a covered container in refrigerator for up to one month. This is perfect on biscuits or plain muffins.

Makes ¾ cup (1 tablespoon per serving)

Nutritional Information per Serving (based on 12 servings)

Calories • 44	Calories from Fat • 0.5	Percent of Calories from Fat • 1%	Fat • 0.1g
Protein • 0.5g	Carbohydrate • 11.6g	Cholesterol • 0mg	Sodium • 2mg

9

BEVERAGES

Mint Julep

Apple-Mint Tea

Lemon-Mint Tea

Ginger-Mint Tea Punch

Mixed Juice Refresher

Pineapple Soda

MINT JULEP

1 sprig fresh mint

1 teaspoon sugar

⅓ cup soda or carbonated
   mineral water

1 shot bourbon

Place fresh mint in a small bowl and crush thoroughly with sugar. Add
soda or mineral water and mash again. Add bourbon, then strain into
a tall, well–chilled glass filled with crushed ice.

Makes 1 drink

Nutritional Information per Serving (based on 1 serving)

Calories • 109	Calories from Fat • 0	Percent of Calories from Fat • 0%	Fat • 0g
Protein • 0g	Carbohydrate • 11.4g	Cholesterol • 0mg	Sodium • 4mg

Apple-Mint Tea

4 tea bags

½ cup fresh mint leaves

2 tablespoons fresh lemon juice

2 cups boiling water

2 cups unsweetened apple juice

4 lemon slices

4 sprigs fresh mint

Combine tea bags, mint leaves, and lemon juice in a pitcher. Pour in boiling water and let stand 10 minutes. Remove and discard tea bags and mint leaves. Stir in apple juice, and serve over crushed ice. Garnish with lemon slices and mint sprigs.

Makes 4 servings

Nutritional Information per Serving (based on 4 servings)

Calories • 62	Calories from Fat • 1	Percent of Calories from Fat • 2%	Fat • 0.2g
Protein • 0.1g	Carbohydrate • 15.7mg	Cholesterol • 0mg	Sodium • 7mg

LEMON-MINT TEA

1 cup boiling water
7 lemon-flavored tea
  bags
2½ tablespoons crushed fresh
  mint leaves

1 6-ounce can frozen lemonade
  concentrate, thawed
1 cup orange juice
7½ cups cold water

Combine boiling water, tea bags, and mint in a large container. Cover
and steep 7 minutes. Remove and discard tea bags. Stir in lemonade,
orange juice, and cold water. Cover and chill 4 to 6 hours. Strain into
ice-filled glasses.

Makes 10 servings

Nutritional Information per Serving (based on 10 servings)

Calories • 47	Calories from Fat • 1	Percent of Calories from Fat • 1%	Fat • 0g
Protein • 0.2g	Carbohydrate • 11.9g	Cholesterol • 0mg	Sodium • 7mg

GINGER-MINT TEA PUNCH

1 2-inch-long piece fresh ginger

2 cups fresh strawberries, chopped fine

½ cup packed fresh mint leaves

4 cups brewed raspberry, cherry, or strawberry tea

2 cups apple juice

12-ounces sparkling mineral water

1 tablespoon finely chopped lemon peel

Cut fresh ginger into fourths. Combine all ingredients and refrigerate 4 to 5 hours to bring out full flavor. Remove and discard ginger pieces. Serve over crushed ice.

Makes 8—10 servings

Nutritional Information per Serving (based on 10 servings)

Calories • 35	Calories from Fat • 2	Percent of Calories from Fat • 5%	Fat • 0.2g
Protein • 0.2g	Carbohydrate • 8.5g	Cholesterol • 0mg	Sodium • 5mg

MIXED JUICE REFRESHER

1 12-ounce can frozen pineapple-orange juice

or

1 12-ounce can frozen cranberry juice

3 12-ounce cans flavored sparkling mineral water

Follow directions on frozen juice can, substituting 1 can of sparkling mineral water for each can of water. Serve over ice. This drink can be any flavor you want. Try unusual combinations for a cool summer treat.

Makes 4—6 servings

Nutritional Information per Serving (based on 6 servings)

Calories • 129	Calories from Fat • 1	Percent of Calories from Fat • 1%	Fat • 0.1g
Protein • 0.9g	Carbohydrate • 31.8g	Cholesterol • 0mg	Sodium • 3mg

PINEAPPLE SODA

1 8–ounce can crushed pineapple
1 pint pineapple sherbet

1½ cups sugar–free ginger ale,
    chilled

Strain pineapple, reserving juice. Divide pineapple juice equally among 4 short, wide glasses. Place 1 scoop of sherbet in each glass, then fill with ginger ale. Top each serving with 2 tablespoons crushed pineapple.

Makes 4 servings

Nutritional Information per Serving (based on 4 servings)

Calories • 166	Calories from Fat • 18	Percent of Calories from Fat • 10%	Fat • 1.9g
Protein • 1.3g	Carbohydrate • 38.1g	Cholesterol • 5mg	Sodium • 46mg

INDEX

allspice, 158
Apple
  –Blueberry Syrup, 160
  Cake, 140
  Fritters, 121
  –Mint Tea, 166
  Pie, Good Old-Fashioned,
    133

Baked Sweet Potatoes, 130
Banana Pancakes, 118
Banana Spice Bread, 136
bay leaf, 8
Beans. *See also* Black-Eyed
    Peas; Green Beans
  Butter, and Rice, 40
  dried, 35
  Kidney, and Chicken,
    69
  Lima, Old-Fashioned
    Baked, 37
  Mississippi, 36
  Pinto, with Turkey Ham,
    44
  Red, and Rice, 41
  White, with Sage, 38
  White, with Turkey, 43
Beef Stock, 8
Bell Peppers. *See* Peppers
Beverages, 165—70
  Apple-Mint Tea, 166
  Ginger-Mint Tea Punch,
    168
  Juice Refresher, Mixed,
    169
  Lemon-Mint Tea, 167
  Mint Julep, 165

  Pineapple Soda, 170
Biscuits. *See also* Bread;
    Muffins; Rolls
  Bran-Buttermilk, 107
  Buttermilk, 105
  Light and Fluffy, 104
  New Orleans Luncheon,
    108
  Sweet Potato, 106
Black-Eyed Pea(s), 9. *See also*
    Beans
  Jambalaya, 42
  and Rice, 39
  Soup, 9
Blackberry Cobbler, 131
Blueberry-Apple Syrup,
    160
Blueberry Dumplings, 145
Bouillabaisse, 12
Bourbon Raisin Sauce (with
    Turkey), 158
Bran-Buttermilk Biscuits,
    107
Bran Muffins, Spiced, 112
Bread. *See also* Biscuits;
    Muffins; Rolls
  Banana Spice, 136
  Corn, 114
  Corn, Chili-Cheese, 115
  Pudding, 144
Broth, Chicken, 7
Burned Fish, 51
Butter Beans and Rice,
    40
Buttermilk Biscuits, 105
Buttermilk-Bran Biscuits,
    107

Cabbage, Down-Home, 94
Cajun
    Catfish Stew, 16
    Chicken and "Dirty" Rice, 67
    Pepper Sauté, 83
    Roux, 153
    Salad, Turkey and Green Bean, 32
    Seasoning Blend, Salt-Free, 149
    Spice Mix, 151
    -Style Haddock, 55
    Zucchini, 98
Cake
    Apple, 140
    Carrot, 138; Cream Cheese Frosting
        for, 138
    Honey, Southern, 139
    Mixed Spice, 142
    Peach Upside-Down, 141
    Pound, 137
    Raisin-Spice Coffee, 143
Candied Sweet Potatoes, 127
Carrot Cake, 138; Cream Cheese
    Frosting for, 138
Casserole
    Potato-Onion, 97
    Sweet Potato, 129
    Yam, 126
Catfish, 52
    Burned Fish, 51
    Creole, Bake, 53
    Étouffée, 50
    Gumbo, 19
    Oven-Fried, 52
    Stew, 17
    Stew, Cajun, 16
Chicken, 47—49
    Breasts, French Quarter, 66
    Broth, 7
    Cajun, and "Dirty" Rice, 67
    Chowder, Country, 15
    Country, 68
    Curry, 71
    Curry Stew, 18
    and Dumplings, 65
    Gravy, 154
    and Kidney Beans, 69
    Oven-Fried, 64
    Pepper, 70

    Smothered, 63
    storing, 48—49
    Vegetable Soup, 13
Chili-Cheese Corn Bread, 115
Chili, Southern, Bonnie's, 24
Chocolate Sauce, Low-Fat, 159
Chowder, Corn, 14
Chowder, Country Chicken, 15
Cinnamon Sauce, Creamy, 157
Cobbler, Blackberry, 131
Cobbler, Peach, 132
Codfish Gumbo, 20
Coffee Cake, Raisin-Spice, 143
Collard Greens, 92
Cookies, Oatmeal, 135
Corn
    Bread, 114
    Bread, Chili-Cheese, 115
    Chowder, 14
    Muffins, 113
    Smothered, 96
Cornmeal, Hush Puppies, 116
Country Chicken, 68
Country Chicken Chowder, 15
Court Bouillon, 5
Crab(meat)
    Cakes, Seasoned, 56
    Salad, 30
    Soup, 10
    and Southern Okra Gumbo, 23
Creole
    Catfish Bake, 53
    Salad, 31
    Stewed Okra and Tomatoes, 86
    Sweet Potato Pone, 134
Crowder Peas, 81
Curry
    Chicken, 71
    Chicken, Stew, 18
    Shrimp, 62

Dessert, 126—45. *See also* Cake
    Apple Pie, Good Old-Fashioned, 133
    Banana Spice Bread, 136
    Blackberry Cobbler, 131
    Blueberry Dumplings, 145
    Bread Pudding, 144
    Candied Sweet Potatoes, 127

Creole Sweet Potato Pone, 134
Oatmeal Cookies, 135
Peach Cobbler, 132
Sweet Potato Casserole, 129
Sweet Potato Pie, 128
Sweet Potatoes, Baked, 130
Yam Casserole, 126
Dessert Sauce
Apple–Blueberry Syrup, 160
Chocolate, Low–Fat, 159
Cinnamon, Creamy, 157
Mock Whipped Cream, 161
Raisin Spread, 162
dietary guidelines, xiii–xiv
Dilled Mustard Sauce, 156
"Dirty" Rice and Cajun Chicken, 67
Down-Home Cabbage, 94
dried beans, 35
Dumplings, 117
Dumplings, Blueberry, 145

egg yolks and egg whites, 125
Eggplant, Stuffed, 95
Étouffée, Catfish, 50
Étouffée, Shrimp, 58

fat, about reducing, xiv–xv
fat in baked goods, 110
filé powder, 22
Fish, 47. See also Catfish
Bouillabaisse, 12
Burned, 51
Codfish Gumbo, 20
Haddock, Cajun–Style, 55
Stock, 6
Trout, Oven-Fried, 54
French Quarter Chicken Breasts, 66
French Toast, Spicy, 120
Fried Green Tomatoes, 88
Fruit, Salad, Southern Morning, 27

Garlic, 66
Ginger Sauce, 155
and Mushrooms, Sautéed, 99
Ginger Garlic Sauce, 155
Ginger-Mint Tea Punch, 168
Gravy, Chicken, 154

Green Bean and Turkey Cajun Salad, 32
Green Beans, Baked, 80
Green Tomatoes, Fried, 88
Greens, Collard, 92
Greens, Turnip, 93
Gumbo, 4, 19
Catfish, 19
Codfish, 20
Quick, 22
Seafood, 21
Southern Okra and Crab, 23

Haddock, Cajun–Style, 55
Honey Cake, Southern, 139
Hush Puppies, 116

Jambalaya, 42
Black–Eyed Pea, 42
Vegetable, 90
Juice Refresher, Mixed, 169

Kidney Beans and Chicken, 69

Lemon–Mint Tea, 167
Lima Beans, Old–Fashioned Baked, 37
Louisiana Seasoning Mix, 150
Louisiana Shrimp Creole, 57
Low–Fat Chocolate Sauce, 159

Mint
–Apple Tea, 166
–Ginger Tea Punch, 168
Julep, 165
–Lemon Tea, 167
Mississippi Beans, 36
Mock Whipped Cream, 161
Muffins. See also Biscuits; Bread; Rolls
Corn, 113
Oatmeal, 111
Spiced Bran, 112
Sweet Potato, 110
Mushrooms and Garlic, Sautéed, 99
Mustard Greens with Turkey Ham, 91
Mustard Sauce, Dilled, 156

New Orleans Luncheon Biscuits, 108
nutmeg, 128

Oatmeal
  Cookies, 135
  Muffins, 111
  Pancakes, 119
Okra, 28
  Creole Stewed, and Tomatoes, 86
  Salad, 28
  Smothered, 85
  Southern, and Crab Gumbo, 23
  Southern Fried, 84
Onion–Potato Casserole, 97
Onions, Pearl, Sautéed, 89
Oven–Fried
  Catfish, 52
  Chicken, 64
  Trout, 54

Pancakes, 119
  Banana, 118
  Oatmeal, 119
Peach Cobbler, 132
Peach Upside-Down Cake, 141
Pearl Onions, Sautéed, 89
Peas, Black–Eyed. *See* Black–Eyed
  Peas
Peas, Crowder, 81
Pepper(s)
  Bell, Turkey-Stuffed, 72
  Bell, Vegetable and Rice—Stuffed,
    82
  Chicken, 70
  Sauté, Cajun, 83
  Shrimp-Stuffed, 60
  Turkey and, 74
Pie, Apple, Good Old-Fashioned,
    133
Pie, Sweet Potato, 128
Pineapple Soda, 170
Pinto Beans with Turkey Ham, 44
Pone, Creole Sweet Potato, 134
Potato(es). *See also* Sweet Potato;
    Yam
  -Onion Casserole, 97
  Salad, 29
poultry. *See* Chicken; Turkey
Pound Cake, 137
Pudding, Bread, 144
Punch, Ginger-Mint Tea, 168

Quick Gumbo, 22

Raisin
  Bourbon Sauce (with Turkey), 158
  -Spice Coffee Cake, 143
  Spread, 162
Red Beans, 41; and Rice, 41
Rice
  Black–Eyed Peas and, 39
  Butter Beans and, 40
  "Dirty," and Cajun Chicken, 67
  long-grain, 57
  Red Beans and, 41
  —Stuffed Bell Peppers, Vegetable
    and, 82
Rolls. *See also* Biscuits; Bread; Muffins
  Easy Dinner, 109
Roux, 153; Cajun, 153

Salad
  Crabmeat, 30
  Creole, 31
  Fruit, Southern Morning, 27
  Potato, 29
  Turkey and Green Bean Cajun, 32
Salsa, Southern, 152
salt, decreasing, xv
Salt–Free Cajun Seasoning Blend, 149
Sauce. *See also* Dessert Sauce
  Bourbon Raisin (with Turkey), 158
  Cajun Roux, 153
  Chicken Gravy, 154
  Dilled Mustard, 156
  Ginger Garlic, 155
  Salsa, Southern, 152
Sausage, Turkey Breakfast, 75
Seafood. *See also* Crab(meat); Fish;
    Shrimp
  Bouillabaisse, 12
  Gumbo, 21
Seasoning
  Blend, Salt-Free Cajun, 149
  Cajun Spice Mix, 151
  Mix, Louisiana, 150
Shrimp, 47
  Creole, Louisiana, 57
  Curry, 62
  Étouffée, 58

Quick and Spicy, 61
Sauté, 59
Soup, 11
–Stuffed Peppers, 60
Smothered
  Chicken, 63
  Corn, 96
  Okra, 85
soul food, xi–xiii
Soup, 5–15. *See also* Chili; Gumbo;
  Stew
  about, 3
  Beef Stock, 8
  Black-Eyed Pea, 9
  Bouillabaisse, 12
  Chicken Broth, 7
  Chicken Chowder, Country, 15
  Chicken Vegetable, 13
  Corn Chowder, 14
  Court Bouillon, 5
  Crab, 10
  Fish Stock, 6
  Shrimp, 11
Southern
  Chili, Bonnie's, 24
  Fried Okra, 84
  Honey Cake, 139
  Morning Fruit Salad, 27
  Okra and Crab Gumbo, 23
  Salsa, 152
Spice(d)
  Bran Muffins, 112
  Bread, Banana, 136
  Cake, Mixed, 142
  Mix, Cajun, 151
  –Raisin Coffee Cake, 143
Spicy French Toast, 120
Spicy and Quick Shrimp, 61
Spread, Raisin, 162
Stew, 3. *See also* Gumbo; Soup
  Cajun Catfish, 16
  Catfish, 17
  Chicken Curry, 18
Stock, 3–4
  Beef, 8
  Fish, 6
Succotash, 87

sugar, decreasing, xv
Sweet Potato(es). *See also* Yam
  Baked, 130
  Biscuits, 106
  Candied, 127
  Casserole, 129
  Muffins, 110
  Pie, 128
  Pone, Creole, 134
Syrup, Apple-Bluebery, 160

Tea
  Apple-Mint, 166
  Lemon-Mint, 167
  Punch, Ginger-Mint, 168
Tomatoes, Creole Stewed Okra and,
  86
Tomatoes, Fried Green, 88
Trout, Burned Fish, 51
Trout, Oven-Fried, 54
Turkey
  Bourbon Raisin Sauce for, 158
  Breakfast Sausage, 75
  and Green Bean Cajun Salad, 32
  Ham, Mustard Greens with, 91
  Ham, Pinto Beans with, 44
  and Peppers, 74
  –Stuffed Bell Peppers, 72
  White Beans with, 43
  Wings and Gravy, 73
Turnip Greens, 93

Vegetable, 80–99. *See also* Name of
  Vegetable
  Chicken Soup, 13
  Jambalaya, 90
  and Rice–Stuffed Bell Peppers, 82
  Succotash, 87

Whipped Cream, Mock, 161
White Beans with Sage, 38
White Beans with Turkey, 43

Yam. *See also* Sweet Potato
  Casserole, 126

Zucchini, Cajun, 98